Are You Still *Mine?*

By Nicole Spencer-Skillen

Copyright © 2021 Nicole Spencer-Skillen

All rights reserved.

No part of this book may be reproduced or used in any manner without the copyright owner's written permission.

This is a work of fiction. Names, characters, places, and incidents either are the product of the author's imagination or are used fictitiously. Any resemblance to actual people, living or dead, events or locales, is entirely coincidental.

First Edition: April 2021

I want to dedicate this novel to everyone that has supported me on my journey so far. Thank you from the bottom of my heart, and I hope you enjoy the story.

CHAPTER ONE

My name is Kacy Sullivan. I live in Raleigh, North Carolina, although I have not lived there my whole life. I was born and raised in Hyde County. With a population of around 6,000, you can imagine how close-knit the community was; with truly little privacy, it was almost impossible to keep anything a secret.

Living in a small community like Hyde meant everybody looked out for each other; the neighbourly closeness made you feel like you belonged. As much as I once complained about everyone knowing every single minor detail of my life, the truth was I missed that place.

We left Hyde County when I was 15 years old. My dad got offered a job in Raleigh as a big-time architect, and the money was just too good to turn down. So, me, mom and my baby brother followed willingly. My baby brother is almost 17 now and around 6'2" with long blonde hair and a bone structure that I envy. Despite this, I still see him as the adorable little three-year-old who used to follow me around everywhere.

Raleigh was a significant change from little old Hyde County. It was a big city, the 42nd most populous in the whole of the United States. A vast 423,000 filled the streets of Raleigh, and I quickly grew to love the city. We lived near the city centre in a suburban town called Willow Springs. Dad's company recommended the area because they built it. Lucky for us, we had the pick of several large five-bedroom houses, several with swimming pools and long gated driveways. Willow Springs was suddenly a fascinating place for me at the age of 15.

After the initial move, I felt like I was dreaming; my bedroom was twice the size of my old one with built-in wardrobes, a king-size bed, and a giant television; I felt like a queen. We had landed on our feet, as my mom would often say.

I went to Magellan Charter Middle School and onto Raleigh Charter High School after that. It was not difficult to make friends in Raleigh. I instantly clicked with a small circle of teenagers my age, and we stuck together through high school and even onto college. Middle school was where I met my best friend, Whitney Sawyer. The first day I saw her, she had a tangled mess of fire-red hair and big gold-rimmed glasses. She rushed through the halls clutching her books to her chest, and I instantly knew we would be friends. If you had seen the shy bookworm she used to be, you would not believe she was now the most confident and beautiful person in the whole city, in my opinion. She had been scouted so often to do modelling jobs or advertisements, but she turned them down every single time because she was studying unbelievably hard to be a lawyer.

We both agreed to go to North Carolina State University after high school; neither of us were particularly keen on the idea of moving across the country. I liked my life in Raleigh. I loved being close to my friends and family, so although I had offers from Duke and Yale, NCSU was easily the first choice for me.

I was studying architectural design as my father did and his brother also. It was something that ran in the family, I guess, but I had taken an interest in it since I could remember. My father would take me on site with him; he would show me plans for new buildings and models of what they would one day become.

It had always seemed like such an exciting job to me growing up, to design a building on paper and then watch it develop into the real thing. I used to see the glow on my dad's face when he would tell us all about the different buildings he had designed. He still does it today, and I picture myself one day doing the same with my children.

University was a fantastic experience. Do not get me wrong, it was difficult, so many late nights and weekends studying, but the eventual outcome always enhanced my motivation further.

To tell a story, I always think you need to go back to the beginning, back to the first moment it all began. That is the only way an accurate picture can be created.

It was the 20th of June 2010, my birthday. The night my life changed, and my eyes truly opened. I was 21 years old; some would say my life was just starting. I was now of a legal age to drink; I could gamble if I felt so inclined, although I never was much of a gambler. I saw what that did to my uncle when I was younger, and it put me off for life.

My birthday was a Saturday that year, which fell perfectly considering all the plans I had for that weekend. Like any other day, I woke at around 8 am to find the sun peeking through my thick crimson curtains. Drawing back the curtains every day to see the view across Willow Springs was still so breathtaking. I had the best view in the house. The moving day consisted of a three-hour stand-off with my brother to make sure I got the house's second most significant room. I was one step away from chaining myself to the radiator until he eventually gave up. I guess you could say I was a handful when I was younger; I knew what I wanted and just how to get it.

As I looked out on that warm summer morning, I could see just about every part of town, including the skyline of Raleigh. Our house was built on high ground, as was the whole estate, perfect if you were one to worry about the frequent heavy rainfall in winter. At sunrise and sunset, it was a truly amazing view.

My phone flashed every few minutes with another happy birthday message or social media notification. After the first five, I opted to switch it to silent. The constant beeping of my phone's generic ringtone was rather irritating after a while. There was one message that caught my eye. A message from Lara.

What can I say about Lara Manning? She was stunning. She had long, flowing blonde hair, accompanied by piercing green eyes and a smile that could light up a room. We had dated for a while in the first year of college, and a part of me thought it could have gone somewhere, but as time went on, we grew apart, and the spark faded. Since the break-up, we bumped into each other occasionally or exchanged the odd text message, but the conversation had evaporated over time.

The text read:

Happy 21st Birthday Kacy!!
I hope you have a fantastic day. It will be nice to see you tonight at Flex. Let me know if you are coming?
I miss you. L x

Flex was an LGBT nightclub in Raleigh; after much debate between my friends and me, it had been the one place we had all mutually agreed on. I had not heard from Lara in almost a year, but that did not change anything between us; there was never any unnecessary awkwardness. I was always happy to see her whenever the moment arose.

When we split, the agreement was that there would be no hard feelings between us. We had many mutual friends, so it was inevitable that we would run into each other on multiple occasions. The fact that she missed me was comforting. It made me smile to know she was still thinking about me.

It was safe to say I had not had any female attention in close to three months, so if something happened between Lara and me, well, my thought exactly was *'what is the harm in that?'* Besides, let's just say she was *hot;* yes, she was undoubtedly hot.

The birthday wishes continued throughout the morning, as well as multiple messages from my best friends, excited for the night ahead. I came downstairs to find my mom, dad, and brother eagerly waiting in the kitchen to present me with cards and gifts. The birthday tradition I looked forward to the most was purely related to food, the smell of pancakes with strawberries, chocolate, and ice-cream radiated from the kitchen. My mom was all about living a healthy lifestyle, so the only day she would willingly make us something so sweet for breakfast was Easter, Christmas, or birthdays.

We always made a considerable effort in our house for birthdays. The fact that it was my 21st made the day even more special. Usually, I would ask my parents for something I so desperately wanted, it would always be reasonably priced, but this year, they insisted that they knew exactly what to get me. There had been one or two surprises over the years; I found keeping the receipts had been the sensible thing to do.

I tried not to ruin the surprise. I knew it would only take $20 and the promise of putting in a good word with one of my friends to get an answer from my brother. Jason hated surprises, he always said so, but you could see the slight disappointment in his face when he found out prematurely what he was getting. That was Jason for you, my impatient and stubborn 'little' brother.

"Good morning, sweetie."

Chirped my mother from across the room. She looked her usual glamorous self in a figure-hugging cream dress accessorised with sparkling diamond earrings and a colossal choker necklace. With shoulder-length blonde hair, blue eyes, and a complexion most would envy, the years had been good to Michelle Sullivan. She had been a model in her younger years and still tried to look her best and keep up with the latest trends even at 52 years of age.

"Happy birthday, sweetheart. I cannot believe my little girl is all grown up."

My dad beamed proudly from ear to ear. He squeezed me so tight that I could barely breathe. I had always been a daddy's girl. He, too, was dressed and ready for work in one of his usual three-piece suits. He had turned 53 a month before my 21st. George Sullivan looked great for his age, his skincare routine was impeccable, and if it were not for the speckles of grey that covered large parts of his hair, he could pass for 40. George was the softer of my parents. I smiled at them both as the third and final figure came towards me.

"Happy birthday, sis. God, you are getting old."

Jason laughed and gave his usual cheeky wink. He always did like to wind me up. We had that kind of relationship where one minute we would be screaming at each other and the next we would be best friends again, but he always had my back, and I had his no matter what.

"Thanks, so much guys. Mom, those pancakes smell delicious."

She had always made the best desserts; that is what made

them so special.

"I know they are your favourite darling. Before you have your breakfast, do you want to see your surprise? Me and your father have kept this a secret for so long now; I don't think we can wait much longer."

There was no need to ask me twice.

"Oh, yes, please, please, please. I can't wait."

My parents both beamed at one another. Michelle led the way, followed by George, who covered my eyes with his hands, wanting the surprise to remain just that until the very last minute.

"Almost there sweetheart, keep your eyes closed...hold on...just a second.... okay, open them."

I was stood in the garage looking at what had to be the most beautiful car I had ever seen; plastered across the hood was a giant red bow and a banner in the background hanging from the garage ceiling read *"Happy Birthday Sweetheart"*. I could not contain my excitement. I passed my driving test two years prior but had always used my mom's car if I needed to go anywhere. I realised after a minute of staring at pure perfection that thanking them had slipped my mind.

"Omg, it is gorgeous. Thank you so, so much. I cannot believe you got me a car!!"

I squealed to the point that my voice was un-recognisable.

"It is an Audi A3; I toyed with an A4, but this model was newer, and it has a bunch of customised elements, like the alloys and the interior. I knew you would want white; it also has a built-in satnav and a system that you can connect your phone to and play your music. Best of all, it's all yours."

My dad loved cars; he knew my favourite car colour was white. He had chosen a white Range Rover the year before because I had insisted on the colour. I could not believe I had my very own car; I was speechless. It was a dream come true and the best birthday present I could have ever wished for.

The rest of the morning and afternoon consisted of me thanking my family repeatedly for all the fantastic gifts I had been given. Not only had I received a car, but my mom had bought me a new laptop. To be completely honest, it was needed more than anything. I was never off my computer; it was so overused I almost felt sorry for it.

My brother had saved up his summer job money to buy me a gorgeous watch. My grandparents surprised me with the trust fund they had saved up for me. Every week for 21 years of my life, they had put five dollars into a private bank account. Over the years, it had equated to an incredible $5500 to spend on whatever I wished. Despite the more practical side of my conscience telling me to use it for something meaningful, the mall was already calling my name.

My 21st birthday was the beginning of the rest of my life; I felt on top of the world. There was always something magical about birthdays, a day when everyone comes together to celebrate one person. It was something I always looked forward to, even more than Christmas. It was not about the presents or the money it was about celebrating with family and friends. My 21st was probably the only day in my whole life that my family and friends were together in the same room, laughing and drinking and generally enjoying life. To me, that was the most important thing. They are the memories that you carry with you forever.

I spent most of my birthday shopping at the mall with Whitney; she was as excited as I was about my new car. We took the bus most days to University, so the prospect of us being able to drive at that time was a huge deal. I had to buy a new outfit for the party later that evening. It took me four shops until I found the perfect dress. A big occasion always called for a new dress. My everyday style was simple—a pair of skinny jeans, sneakers and a t-shirt. I was not the type to bring out the 6-inch heels unless it was necessary. Comfort was key. The dress I found came with a hefty price tag of $300. Usually, I would spend around $50, but I told myself it was necessary. I would only be 21 once. After buying a new bag, matching shoes, two new pairs of sneakers and a pair of skinny jeans, the bill totalled around $700. We made one last pit stop at our local coffee shop for an iced mocha. My favourite drink in one hand and my shopping in the other, it was time to head home.

The party was projected to start at around 7 pm. I had suggested having it at home instead of hiring a venue. We had a spacious house with more than enough room to accommodate. Our backyard was well equipped to host at least 50 people. My mom had recently bought a brand-new set of outdoor furniture and a jacuzzi, so why not put it to fair use were my initial thoughts.

My mom hired a caterer, and I asked a local DJ that I knew from NCSU to provide the music; he was more than happy to play for free if he could video the whole event to post on his social media pages. The house was trimmed up with balloons, banners, and, of course, in true Sullivan tradition, many old embarrassing photos. As I wandered through the house, there was one excruciatingly painful picture after another; the old photo albums had been put to good use. I told myself I would later punish my mother for those.

Everyone knew where I lived, and it was easy to access for all my family and friends. So, home had seemed like the perfect place to host my party. People started to arrive at around 6 pm. I was slightly behind schedule as Michelle kindly reminded me with every person that came.

"Sweetheart, you need to hurry. Your guests are arriving."

I could tell from her tone of voice she was unwilling to

entertain my friends herself, so the quicker I got ready, the better.

"Two minutes, mom. I am just finishing my hair."

Okay, so that was the third time I had said that, but my hair was difficult to tackle some days. I had a generous head of golden brown hair which untamed looked bushy and unkept, and a bad hair day on my 21st birthday would not have been acceptable. The eye shadow of choice was a toned down natural nude that worked wonders for my chestnut coloured eyes, or so I had been told. I had Whitney to thank for my latest make-up additions.

Once I was fully ready, the party truly started. My friends and family arrived one by one. They all took it in turn to tell embarrassing stories about me and laugh at the photos around the house. I was showered with even more cards and gifts. The dining room table had been the nominated present area, and it was almost full before the last few guests were due to arrive.

"Wow, birthday girl. Who knew you were so popular?"

That was my best friend's voice. Whitney pulled me in for a hug whilst blatantly pointing towards the large present to the right of the table. It was wrapped beautifully in my favourite colours, orange and white. A huge orange bow decorated the front perfectly.

"That one is from me, but you cannot open it until tomorrow. I want to see your face."

"Wow, I am intrigued; I hope you are not getting me back for my empty box trick last year."

I smirked at the thought, the entertainment value of that trick would never get old.

"Would I ever? I did think about it for a second actually; then I remembered I am not as cruel as you."

"Very funny, you loved it. By the way, there is absolutely no way that you wrapped that present yourself."

"I so did!!"

She shrieked. The grin on her face said otherwise.

"Seriously, you made me re-wrap all your Christmas presents for you last year because your attempt looked like a child had been let loose with some sticky tape and glitter."

We both laughed hysterically because she knew how true that was. Whitney was good at a lot of things, but she was terrible at wrapping.

"Okay, smart ass, so I didn't wrap it myself, but I watched some handsome guy wrap it for me instead. I think I might save you a job this year and go back to get all my Christmas presents done."

She was hilarious. The things she would do to get a guy's attention was beyond what any reasonably sane person would do; I had to love her for it though.

"Oh, great. I sure hope he doesn't quit before the year is out then. That will save me a lot of time."

"Let's hope not! Anyway, is it time to go yet? I am so excited."

"I can tell, you are like a new-born puppy."

I laughed and pushed her towards the crowded living room.

"I need to do some more mingling, so you, my beautiful best friend, need to occupy your time."

I shouted after her as I left the room, giggling to myself, "Try not to pee on anything" It took her a few seconds before she realised that I was referencing the puppy dog statement; in return, I got the middle finger.

Everyone started to leave around 10 pm, but the party was only just beginning for my friends and me. The clubs in Raleigh ultimately the next stop.

Me, Whitney, and Savannah all jumped into my father's car. My other friends Jake, Jessica, Ryan, and Sophia, jumped in with my mom. Neither of my parents liked to drink a lot of alcohol; one glass of white wine or a whiskey would usually be the extent of it. So, they often voluntarily became designated drivers.

Saturday the 20th of June had been pencilled in on the calendar for a long time. My friends and I had saved every spare penny for months in anticipation of a night out we would never forget. We had already purchased wristbands and paid for VIP seating in the best clubs. Champagne was on tap, kindly purchased by my parents. I was the youngest of my group of friends; they were between the ages of 21 and 24. There was now me, Whitney and Jennifer that shared the tender age of 21.

My 21st was set up to be the best night out I had ever experienced. I required no more fake ID, no more under 21 parties, and no more illegal drinking. The world was my oyster; it was time to start living it, finally I thought.

The night was set to be excellent; first, we went to Flex. I felt like a celebrity. We had VIP passes and a particular seated VIP area reserved just for us. There were 13 of us that started the evening, but by the time we moved to Club Fifteen, shortly after midnight, there were around 25 people in our VIP box. Savannah, Sophia, and Whitney were making it known just how single they were as the night progressed, often dragging random boys into the cordoned-off area that we occupied.

Whitney especially was newly single, so you could not blame her for the three handsome guys she had invited over. I looked forward to seeing how she would get out of that one, with all three of them vying for her attention.

Between 1 am and 2 am, Club Fifteen was the place to be. That is when it started to get busy. The queue to get in was over 40 people long by the time we got there. The chances of getting in were slim to none because not many people wanted to leave once inside. Luckily for us, we had planned the evening for a long time. Much to the envy of everyone who stood in line, we placed our queue-jumping passes in the hands of the doorman. It took no longer than twenty seconds for us to be inside.

The atmosphere was incredible; Club Fifteen had been renovated two years prior to look like something straight out of New York City. Inside the hardwood flooring was solid oak; plush red carpets covered the walkways giving you the feeling you were on the red carpet at the Grammy's. The fake paparazzi stood by the entrance with state-of-the-art cameras added to the effect. The type of cameras that do not add 10 pounds, instead they made you look like America's next top model. Finally, it was the lighting that sealed the deal. Dark, seductive, and sensual across all three floors. I could not get enough of the place.

There were three different bars, one purely just for cocktails, several dance floors, each with a different theme and DJ. Best of all, if you were to head right to the top floor, you would find balconies overlooking the whole of Raleigh. Not only was the view incredible, but throw in a few palm trees, a gorgeous seating area, and a bartender on hand. That gave you the most beautiful place to relax and drink in the whole of the city. I had the privilege of being on that top floor, having the time of my life with the people I loved.

My best friends in the whole world by my side and drinks on tap equalled perfection.

What I was about to experience next was an unexpected gift.

CHAPTER TWO

On my right, I caught a glimpse of her amongst a crowd of people, yet she stood out so effortlessly. I was perched at the bar ordering what would have been my third martini.

The bartender had also made his third attempt at flirting with me, not wanting to get into the whole *'I'm gay'* conversation. I simply just smiled politely and paid for my drink.

I do not know what made me look twice in her direction; maybe it was the sound of her laugh that caught my attention, but something inside me wanted to look over again, and when I did, I could not look away.

First, I saw her eyes. They were such a powerful blue that even though I was halfway across the room, I was mesmerised by them. Her loosely curled brown hair fell just above her shoulders and her teeth were so clear to see when she laughed. They were perfect in every way, the kind of teeth you assume must be veneers, but some people are just blessed with. She had olive skin and a slim, toned body. It could be seen perfectly through her grey, ripped, skinny jeans and the tight, white t-shirt she wore under her leather jacket. At first, her sexual orientation was not clear, but then she looked back at me. I must have made it evident that I was staring at her, but she did not look away much to my surprise.

I followed her eyes as she took in every inch of me. My hair, my dress, my legs. She eyed every part of my body with a diminutive smile on her face, and then she whispered in her friend's ear before starting towards me.

Instantly I froze, unsure how to react. Would she ask me why I was staring at her? What would I say? I did what any regular person would do, and hastily turned away towards the bar. At that moment, the only thought I could comprehend was how much I needed a mirror. The need to check my make-up, my hair and my teeth was paramount. There was nothing worse than talking to someone you found attractive, then realising afterwards you had something stuck in your teeth. Trust me, I am speaking from experience.

"Hey, I'm Alex."

There was a minor pause on my behalf. I was nervous beyond belief. I took her in for a second as she spoke to me; she was even more striking up close. Her voice was so husky and seductive. She had confidence and charisma that radiated from every part of her body.

"Hi, I'm Kacy."

I could not think of anything witty or intelligent to say. I was a confident person usually, but at that moment, my vocabulary deserted me. I ordered myself to keep it together.

"I like that name. Nice to meet you, Kacy. I saw you earlier buying a martini; they must be good?"

That made me feel slightly better, knowing she had seen me before I had seen her. Maybe she had been watching me too.

"Yes, they are my favourite. Can I get you one? You will not regret it."

I declared.

"I already have a drink at my table, but maybe next time? Is it your birthday today?"

"Yes, how did you know?"

I was mesmerized by the entirety of what she said. I wanted to keep her talking for as long as I could. Every word that formulated on her lips was so intense, and I could not work out if that came naturally or if she was trying to be that way. Either way, I liked it.

"You were the girl who stood in the middle of all those people over there when they sang happy birthday to you? Also, the big badge attached to your bag kind of gives it away."

She expressed with a smirk on her face; she obviously found that amusing. I failed to remember the gigantic badge Whitney had forced me to wear. It had to remain on some part of my attire for the whole evening. Those were the rules. I had gone extremely red and embarrassed when all my friends decided to sing to me; it seems that was something else she had observed that evening.

"Yes, unfortunately, that was me. My friends like to show me up. I see you found that entertaining."

I rolled my eyes flippantly.

"Very…so Kacy, I really should get back over to my friends. I don't want to seem too forward, but could I maybe take your number and see you again sometime?"

She leant up against the bar, looking directly into my eyes when she spoke. The girl gave me butterflies with every word that materialised from her flawless lips. I did not want her to leave; there was something inside my body yearning to get to know her more.

"Sure, I would like that. Are you leaving? Or do you and your friends want to come upstairs to the balcony?"

I was hoping with every inch of me she would say yes. I had known her for five minutes, but the connection between us was electrifying.

"If I come up to the balcony with you, you have to promise

me one thing?"

She said with a modest smile that made the side of her mouth curl up in such a flirtatious manner.

"What would that be?" I replied.

I desperately tried my best to be even half as sexy as Alex was, whilst hoping she did not notice the palpable effect she was having on me.

"You have to promise that after tonight is over, I get to take you somewhere for breakfast? I know the perfect place."

How could I say no to that? I am not sure if it was the ever-growing intoxication I was under or the sheer mystery of the woman stood before me. She could have hauled me anywhere she wanted. I do not think I would have distrusted it.

"I would love that; breakfast sounds great."

The grin that engulfed my face was unmistakable, but I had the feeling she often provoked that response in women. Alex strolled back to her table and informed her friends of the change in plans. Although I made it clear her friends were more than welcome to join us, she quickly shut the idea down on her return, saying that they much preferred to be on the middle floor where they currently resided. That is where the DJ played base music and that was their favourite. So, it seemed she was riding solo; I was not about to complain. We immediately re-joined my friends and once we advanced to the balcony, I introduced her.

"Alex, this is Whitney, my best friend and this is Savannah and Jennifer. Guys, this is Alex."

The rest of the group introduced themselves one by one, making her feel more than welcome. I knew they would be so polite when I presented them to Alex, which made it comfortable and stress-free on my part, considering I still was not entirely sure what the rest of the evening would bring. That did make it even more appealing.

Whitney pulled me to one side after the onslaught of introductions.

"Wow, Kace, I mean well done. Where did you pull that one from? She seems great."

"I know, right? Too good to be true at this point!"

"Nothing is too good to be true Kace, embrace it."

She squeezed my arm before hurrying off to join her entourage of men. When I looked back over to see Alex's whereabouts, it seemed as though she had the approval of all my friends. They crowded around her as she so easily commanded their attention.

I desired to get to know her better. I strolled over and pulled her to the far corner of the balcony, away from prying eyes. I was mindful that it was my birthday and all my friends were there for me, but I was compelled to get to know her, and I knew they would understand.

We conversed for over an hour about everything. I found out so much about her. Her full name was Alex Lorena Dawson. The middle name was given to her in remembrance of her great grandmother, which she was swift to point out. Personally, I thought it was lovely.

She was 23 years old and had never attended College. Instead, she had taken a job in her parents' bar upon leaving school. The bar which she now owned with her sister Natalie, she informed me that her parents had passed away in a catastrophic car accident two years earlier. I was shocked and saddened to hear that news, but she did not for a second make the conversation uncomfortable or want me to feel remorseful for her. The ease in which she spoke about it made it evident that she had come to terms with the tragedy, as hard as that must have been.

Alex had lived in Raleigh her whole life, but it only required an hour-long conversation to realise that she had intentions to travel the world. The concept of opening a bar in Europe seemed to fascinate her and was a dream she anticipated she would one day achieve.

"Where in Europe would you like to open a bar?"

Alex responded confidently and swiftly.

"That is easy, definitely Italy. Italian culture has always fascinated me."

"Have you ever been to Italy?"

She took a sip of her drink before responding.

"Only once, with my parents when me and Natalie were a bit younger. We went to Rome and Milan. What about you?"

"I have sadly never been, but I would love to one day. Especially Rome, I bet it's incredible?"

Alex looked out to the landscape across Raleigh. It was a picturesque night; the music was low and serenading, creating an ambience like no other. She motioned for me to look towards the skyline.

"Look's beautiful, doesn't it? We sometimes forget just how lucky we are to be able to experience sights like that. And Rome, well, it is a feeling I cannot explain. It is so ancient but so beautiful at the same time. I will go back one day to experience it as an adult. I felt like I did not appreciate the culture at the age of seventeen."

We both gazed up at the stars in unison, merely taking it all in. She made me feel so at ease.

"Really beautiful."

I think she realised I was not solely referring to the skyline.

The night came to a close at around 3 am when the bartender called out for last orders. I had sobered entirely after chatting with Alex for over two hours. My friends had left at different intervals throughout the evening until the last two remaining were Jessica and Jake, the cutest couple I knew. They had been together for three years and always relished a good night out. They too, eventually said their final goodbyes. My attention quickly turned back to Alex as she stood and prepared herself to leave.

"So, are you ready for breakfast?"

Alex held out her hand to assist me in getting off the barstool that I had so comfortably been perched on for most of the evening.

"What like right now? It's 3 am. Who serves breakfast at 3 am?"

I was bemused. I thought she had intended we go for breakfast the next day, at least after I had gone home, slept and changed into something more relaxing.

"Yes, like right now. The best time to go for breakfast is after a night out. You have no idea how hungry alcohol makes me. I am going to take you to a place that does the best pancakes in the whole of North Carolina."

There was no need to ask me twice; not a solitary bone in my body wanted to go home to bed. Being with her made me feel so alive.

The diner Alex took me to was a 10-minute walk away from Club Fifteen. It was named Early Bird Diner, and it opened at 3 am every single day. The only people in there were truckers at that time in the morning, making a pit stop before hitting the road again. The diner was hidden away, screened by large wooden fences which supported the fact that I had never caught a glimpse of it before that day, but then again, I did not venture to downtown Raleigh very often.

I studied the diner as we entered; it was tattered and shabby but quirky. Despite the interior, I was reassured promptly that the kitchen area was immaculate. Alex steered me towards a booth located at the back.

"How long has this place been here?"

"Oh god, I don't know actually, a long time though, my dad used to bring me here."

I picked up the coffee stained A4 piece of paper that operated as a menu, but Alex speedily took it from my hands.

"Allow me; I know the perfect order."

After I nodded in agreement, she sauntered off and returned moments later with two drinks in hand.

"I have ordered us both chocolate chip pancakes with maple syrup, vanilla whipped cream, and strawberries on the side. Trust me when I say you will love them."

She was beaming with self-confidence.

"How did you know what to order? Of all the things you could have ordered, and you chose my favourite pancakes."

"They are the best thing on the menu. If I am completely honest, I have tried most things on that menu, and believe me; they are the only thing worth having."

"Is that right? Just a lucky choice from you then." I smirked.

The pancakes arrived within minutes; the first bite was one of pure perfection. Alex watched as my face turned from ordinary to pure enjoyment.

"How was that?"

Alex knew the answer to that question. I could only presume she wanted the satisfaction of hearing me say it.

"I like your taste in food."

The words came out stifled in between the mouthfuls of pancake I consumed at a rapid rate.

"I told you didn't I? It's a hidden gem. I am glad you are enjoying it."

I was becoming conscious of how I must have appeared; I had not topped up my make-up for almost four hours, and there was the pancakes that I crammed unapologetically into my mouth. Not a good combination.

"I am, so thank you so much for bringing me here. It is the

perfect end to my birthday."

The company made it more so than the actual food, but I left that part out.

"It is my pleasure, Kacy."

The silence loitered briefly as we consumed the remainder of our breakfast.

"So how is someone like you single?"

It was a question I was desperate to know the answer to.

Surely, she had to have some flaws that had not been made apparent on meeting her.

"The same reason someone like you is still single."

"Who said I am single?"

I raised my eyebrows; Alex expressed great amusement.

"Funny you should say that. I thought the girl to your left with the long blonde hair was your girlfriend. That was until I caught you looking back at me, then I assumed I must have been wrong."

She was referring to Lara. She had been firmly by my side for at least the first hour of the evening, but I did not feel we looked overly cosy.

"Ahh, you are talking about Lara. No, not together, or I would not be here with you now, would I. Long story short though, we did date in college, but we are purely just friends now."

Alex pursed her lips in a way that made me think she was reluctant to rely on my side of the story.

"You could have fooled me. You should tell her that."

She was brazen and I liked that.

"Anyway, stop changing the subject. I asked why you were single."

Alex contemplated the idea, maybe unsure on how much to divulge at that stage.

"I am yet to find the right girl. There are no skeleton's in my closet, if that's what you're thinking. I guess sometimes things just don't work out."

She shrugged it off.

"I agree."

We spoke for another hour; the conversation was seemingly effortless—something I was not accustomed to.

"I have really enjoyed tonight Alex, all of it."

No amount of coffee was going to keep me awake much longer. The evening's events were finally catching up to me.

"I have too. I can walk you home if you are ready to go? The sun will be rising shortly and that is the best part."

There was a twinkle in her eye; neither one of us wanted the night to end.

"I mean, in theory, I would love that, but it might take a while; I live in Willow Springs."

The walk from Downtown Raleigh to Willow Springs would have taken two hours. Initially, I had arranged a minibus to pick my friends and me up from outside Icon, but that was at 4 am. It was supposed to be taking me, Whitney, and Sophia back to my house, but it was now 5 am, my friends had gone home, and I was with Alex. I thought about calling my mom, she would not be pleased about me disrupting her beauty sleep, but I was her only daughter, so I was convinced she would get over it. Just as I pondered the dilemma I found myself in, Alex suggested an alternative that I found too alluring to turn down.

"You could come back to mine then? I only live around the corner from here. You can crash until later today, and when I have slept off the alcohol, I can take you home."

Going home with a stranger after a night out was new to me, but that night felt different. Uncommon in the sense that I did not feel like I was going somewhere with a stranger, I did not feel uncomfortable at the prospect of sleeping at her place. I had this all-consuming calmness about me like I knew she would take care of me.

"Are you sure you don't mind? It would be a lot easier."

She looked down at her feet, then back up at me, and responded without hesitation.

"Not at all. Follow me. It's not far."

We set off walking towards her apartment. I was keen to take in the surrounding area, having never been to her neighbourhood before. We passed her bar along the way; it was called Dawson's Grill & Bar. I was sure I had seen it before in passing but never had I been inside. I recalled a few of my friends highlighting it as the new place to go before hitting the nightclubs. I thought to myself, I would soon have to see what all the fuss was about.

"I will show you inside some time. We had it refurbished late last year, so it has a whole new feel to it. Most people have taken to it well, so I think you will like it."

I had resisted flirting excessively for most of the night/early morning. I had always been under the impression that you had to leave something to the imagination. Never give too much away. I was sure by me just being there that Alex knew she was of interest to me on some level, but a feeling inside told me to make it unmistakable.

"If you are going to be there, what is there not to like?"

She smirked and blushed ever so slightly.

We arrived at Alex's apartment after walking for five minutes; I was taken aback by just how wonderful it was. She explained that both she and her sister sold the family home outside of Raleigh after her parents passed. They decided to buy two apartments in the downtown area closer to the bar and their grandparents. Her apartment was on the top floor. It had a spectacular open plan living area with brick walls and a solid wood kitchen. The character of the two bedrooms was impressive, both with built-in wardrobes and king-size beds.

The whole apartment had a charm that made you instantly fall in love with it. The best part was the full length, floor to ceiling glass windows; they opened out onto a rooftop expanse with remarkable views of the city.

The views that I appreciated so much on Club Fifteen's balcony, the ones I had bragged about that evening for over ten minutes, were, in fact views she had conveniently in her own apartment. The fanatical thing being, hers were even better. The apartment building was considerably higher up, which allowed for every part of the breath-taking landscape to be seen.

"I cannot believe you let me rant on about the view from the balcony when you have this amazing view right here!"

I stood peering through the glass panes in awe. Alex expressed her own amusement before replying.

"Well, to be honest, I just liked listening to you talk. Several times tonight you have described a view or a building and how you talk about them, it is fascinating to me. I mean, I just see them as buildings; I do not look as deep into it as you do. I can tell you are going to be a fantastic architect; you have such a passion for this stuff."

I wondered again if she was just too good to be true.

"Do you want a drink?"

Alex waltzed off towards the fridge.

"I would love some water please; my mouth is so dry."

"No problem, filtered okay? I have no bottles left, I'm afraid."

I glared over in her direction before blatantly rolling my eyes.

"Tap water is fine with me, honestly. I am not posh."

She returned to the lounge area two minutes later with an ice-cold glass of water. She handed me the glass and ushered me out onto the balcony.

"It is almost sunrise, and I guarantee it is the best thing you will ever experience from up here, I promise you. If I ever need any sort of inspiration, I sit right here first thing on a morning and just watch the world wake up. It reminds me of how lucky we are."

I was always open to a new experience.

"You are aware that this is the second time tonight you have introduced me to one of the best things I will ever experience? Twice in one night, you are giving yourself a lot to live up to here."

Alex turned towards me, sporting an incredibly charming smile.

"And the nights not even over yet." She winked.

My face flushed at once.

We both sat in silence as the sun came up in the distance, neither of us needing to speak to fill any space between us. She placed her hand on mine, and my eyes moved away from the sun to meet hers. There was no awkward silence that you might encounter on a first date. I had been there before when you run out of things to say. It was unique with her; I would go as far as saying, utter perfection. There were no small exchanges of chitter-chatter, no need for entertainment to cure any boredom; there simply was no boredom. As I looked into her eyes and the sun came up, the feeling was so intense and so passionate. I felt as though I had known her my whole life.

Alex read the signals exceptionally well. She must have known by the way I slowly edged my body towards hers. It took her no time at all to pluck up the courage to kiss me. She placed the palm of her hand upon my cheek, and upon her lips coming together with mine, I felt electricity surge through my body. Our lips fit effortlessly together, which was something I had never experienced before. The rhythm in which we moved our lips was seamlessly synchronised, almost like they had met in the past. I closed my eyes and fell profoundly into a kiss that would change my life.

The kisses became harder and more intense. The craving and the sexual tension between us was otherworldly. It was inevitable what would follow, but it would not just be a one-night stand. It would not be just sex. It would be captivating; I knew that before it happened. I could feel it with every bone in my body. The way she kissed my neck and caressed my skin so delicately grew more formidable with every movement.

I had never felt so attractive, so wanted and needed like the way she made me feel. The way she yearned for my body and hungered for my touch, just as I did for her. We realised that the balcony was not private enough for an encounter like ours, so Alex guided me to the bedroom.

The second that the door closed behind us, her lips met mine once again. I rotated and pressed my body up against hers, which backed the foot of the bed. Alex slowly unzipped my dress so effortlessly. As the dress slipped down my uncovered frame, I felt her hands run down my back and stop at my hips. I turned and sat on the edge of the bed. Alex pulled her t-shirt over her head and unzipped her jeans whilst I took in her extraordinary physique. It was just the right balance between slim and toned; she was pleasing to the eye. I pulled Alex towards me as I lay back on the bed, inviting her to rub her body up against mine. The sensation was overwhelming as we intertwined our bodies. She knew exactly what she was doing and left nothing to the imagination.

The night finally came to a close at around 8 am, when we both fell to sleep in each other's arms, completely and utterly exhausted. I felt so peaceful and untroubled. My final thought was a reference to Alex's earlier comment; She had been right. I had just experienced the third best thing since meeting her.

I knew my friends would think I was bizarre; it was human nature to react in that way. After all, who claim's they feel so infatuated after only knowing someone for a mere eight hours. It is not something I could do justice in explaining. The truth, it is a sentiment not comprehended unless you have had the pleasure of experiencing it.

People want to believe in love at first sight, they want to believe in epic love stories that begin and end like the movies, but that is not always the case. I could tell you that the moment I met Alex, fireworks spontaneously erupted in the night sky. I could tell you that our eyes locked, and right then, we fell hopelessly and truly in love.

That, however, was not the case, but our first acquaintance was one of perfection. We laughed, we smiled, and we talked through to sunrise and on after that. Everything between us was undeniably natural and genuine, like we had been doing it our whole lives. It may not have been love at first sight, but it was a desire at first sight; it was attraction and intensity beyond any reasonable doubt that was clear to see, but love at first sight?

I believe, until proven wrong that it is merely a myth created for humankind so that we can believe in a love like no other, but what we had was even better.

It was real, and it certainly was set in stone to be epic.

CHAPTER THREE

I woke dazed from a sleep that had absorbed me completely. An incessant buzzing bewildered me instantly.

What was that?

I turned to my left to see Alex; happiness overwhelmed me. It had not all been some elusive dream, relief. I turned towards the buzzing to discover my phone on the cabinet against the far wall. My phone stopped vibrating, I went to lay back down, but it immediately started up again. Someone really wanted to get in contact with me. Once I reached my phone, it was Whitney's name flashing on the screen. I answered with a sheepish hello.

"KACY!!! Are you okay?"

How she shrieked my name was painful to the ear.

"Of course I'm okay."

Why was she so irate? My initial thought.

"Why are you so casual? Do you realise what stress you have put me under? Where have you been all day? I was one phone call away from calling the police."

The room was a dusky black, I assumed it was because the curtains were drawn, but as I walked towards the window, I realised it was dark outside.

What time was it? The clock on the wall must have been

wrong. It could not have been 8 pm. My thoughts exactly.

"I'm sorry, Whit. I swear I did not realise the time. We only fell to sleep at around 8 am. I cannot believe I have slept until now."

There was only one part of my loose explanation that she focused on.

"We?"

I recognised swiftly that I had some explaining to do.

"I have been with Alex. It is a lot to discuss right now, but I am okay."

There was a brief pause on the line.

"Okay, first of all, do not ever do that to me again. I started to get worried. Your mom text me because she called you earlier and got no answer. I just told her you had gone back to bed to sleep off your hangover and I would get you to call her when you woke up."

Alex started to arouse.

"I will not do it again, I promise. Thank you for always having my back. I will call my mom in a minute."

"I need the full low down on absolutely everything you got up to once you get home. It better be juicy considering all the worry you have put me through today."

We quickly ended the conversation with a swift goodbye, and I proceeded to reply to the string of messages from my mom. I told her I had been at Whitney's all day and I would be home soon. That would suffice. I turned back towards the bed to see Alex sat up against the headboard. It was completely dark in the bedroom bar one stream of light coming from the bathroom door being left ajar, creating a perfect silhouette of Alex.

"Good morning, everything okay?"

She had not realised the time either.

"Good evening, you mean, it's 8 pm."

I strolled back towards the bed to join her if she was not distracting enough, the reality of her being topless certainly added to it.

"Seriously? I was out for the count, was that your friend calling?"

She pulled the cover back and motioned for me to get in beside her.

"Me too, better than I have slept in a long time. It was Whitney, she was freaking out for a second, but she is okay now she knows she doesn't need to explain my disappearance to the police department."

Alex chuckled, putting her arm out for me to bury my head in her chest. I felt remarkably content. I was in no rush to end what had been undoubtedly one of the best nights of my life.

"It's a good job you woke up when you did then. I had a great time last night, by the way."

She revealed the last part quietly. She did not strike me as the shy type.

"It was the best. Thank you so much Alex."

"Thank you for what?"

I paused momentarily before clarifying.

"The past 24 hours. All of it. It has been a dream."

Alex leant down and lifted my chin towards her. She delicately placed her lips against mine; I shut my eyes and imagined a world where those lips met mine every single day. That was a world worth thinking about. I did not go home that night. The chance to stay with Alex and relive the night before was all I could contemplate. Much to my satisfaction, she did not want me to leave.

The following days passed by so quick, I went home for an hour, purely to pack some clothes and then I swiftly headed back to Alex's apartment. My parents were none the wiser. I informed them that I had decided to stay at Whitney's for a few days; that was not something out of the ordinary. The number of times I had gone to Whitney's and not re-appeared for at least a week was countless. I wanted the chance to explore whatever it was me and Alex had recently discovered, without the pressure that loomed when friends and parents became aware.

We spent every waking minute we had together. I found myself reluctant to leave her, just in case it had all been a dream, a cruel dream that was dangling her perfection in front of me, only to take it back and claim it as a nightmare instead.

I became quickly aware after two days that I had a life outside of the bubble we created for ourselves and University was the first port of call. My final exams were only around the corner and the degree of studying they would require for me to pass was nothing short of incalculable. Alex had her usual work routine; she called in a favour with her sister so we could spend the day after my 21st birthday together, but then she had to return to normality, and every second in between, we could not stay away from each other.

Never had I looked so fiercely towards every sunrise, eagerly awaiting a new day, knowing that I would soon see her again. She was like a book I never wanted to put down, a best seller with torn pages and coffee stains. I wanted to keep reading, delving in deeper to find out every detail about who she was. I sought to discover the countless adventures and experiences she had once been a part of. She fast became my addiction.

It was a humid night in early July. The balcony of Alex's apartment had become my writing haven. A place so tranquil, so full of inspiration as Alex had conveyed on the night we met. I was nearing the final page of my Journal, and what a way it was due to end. There was something stimulating about keeping a journal; I had done it since I was 12 years old. I would go months at a time without writing, but then I would often stumble upon the inspiration I was looking for, which in turn would throw me right back into the pages of my life. I took pleasure in knowing that one day when my memories deserted me, I would be able to recall the events as if it was only yesterday.

"What are you writing?"

I jumped, startled. Alex snuck up so stealthily it took me by surprise. I hadn't heard her arrive home. She leant over the back of the chair and kissed my forehead from above. A small comfort that warmed me to the core.

"You scared me! You are back early? Quiet evening?"

Alex pulled up the chair beside me whilst giggling to herself, still amused by my reaction.

"Sorry! I couldn't resist. Yes, really quiet actually; Natalie's got the evening covered."

She drew her chair closer to mine and pulled my legs comfortably over hers—a position we found ourselves in most evenings.

"Well, I am glad you're back. I was just thinking about ordering some food. I assume it's okay for me to stay here again tonight?"

Did your parents ever tell you that you should not assume? I must have neglected to pay attention to that lesson. Alex had not asked me to leave in over a week, but I did fear that I was making myself too comfortable.

"You don't need to ask. I told you that already. I love having you here."

Phewww.

"I was hoping you would say that. Mainly because of this view, though. It has nothing to do with you."

She pinched my leg playfully.

"So you have still failed to tell me what you are writing in that journal of yours. I hope it's about me."

I placed my pen to one side and closed the journal.

"That is for me to know. You cannot expect a girl to express her deepest and darkest thoughts."

Alex grinned mischievously and reached for the journal. My swift reactions winning easily.

"Come on! That's not fair. Let me have a sneak peek. How about you read me a few lines?"

I contemplated the idea. The last entry was about her, but the vulnerability that came with revealing it was daunting.

"Okay, if I read you a few lines, can we drop it and go order some food?"

Alex nodded enthusiastically. I opened my journal back up to the last active page. I was in danger of being exposed unless she too could resonate with the words I wrote.

"There are stars that shine bright and a moon that keeps the planet alight. There are solitary birds that sing an impeccable tune and vibrant flowers that always bloom. Everywhere you look, there is beauty, but sometimes it takes a particularly special moment, a rare sight or an exceptional person to help us appreciate what we had ignored for so many years. The art, the creativity, the sounds, the colours, the smells, and even the imperfections we long to hide. There is beauty everywhere I look and I realise now, you were all it took."

Alex removed the journal from my hands and leant forward to bring her lips to mine. Her initial reaction unpredicted.

"Honestly, that was beautiful. Do you have any other talents I should know about?"

I softly brushed the loose strand of blonde hair behind her ear.

"Well, you will just have to wait and see won't you."

I wondered if she knew that she was my muse?

Emerging from my love bubble a week later, I realised I had been extremely anti-social. I had only briefly spoken to the girls since my birthday night, we had a group chat, and they were eagerly awaiting answers to all their inappropriate questions. I arranged to meet Whitney, Jessica, and Sophia for lunch on campus after my first written examination. It was a good job I had paid extra attention throughout the year; the added benefit of having a dad who was also an architect helped. Let's just say my mind had been elsewhere in the week leading up to the exam, but I was quietly confident none the less.

I made my way to the central campus. The food choices were vast as always, I usually would opt for a salad, but as soon as the smell of fresh, stone-baked pizza hit me, there was no doubt in my mind what I would be having for lunch.

Jessica had been the first to arrive and had successfully saved us a table by the window.

"Hi Jess, you okay?"

I leant over the chair closest to the window to embrace her.

"Kacy! It's so good to see you girl. How did the exam go?"

I draped my bag on the chair, took a seat beside her, and exhaled a long overdue sigh of relief.

"Average, you know what it's like. I am trying not to overthink it."

Jessica smiled ironically.

"Please, you are one of the cleverest people I know. You will have killed it, I am positive."

"Thanks. Time will tell."

Just as Jess reached for her soda, a shriek from behind made us both jolt.

"Kacy Michelle Sullivan! She has risen from the dead!"

Whitney marched around the table and placed herself firmly on the chair opposite me. Sophia followed, laughing to herself at Whitney's overzealous entrance. There was a brief nod in acknowledgement of each other, knowing full well that I was about to get interrogated.

"Why are you so dramatic? It has literally been a week!"

I playfully threw a napkin in her direction. I knew she would pretend to be offended, but I also knew her better than anyone else in the world; it would not last.

"FYI, it has been two weeks, at least, and what makes it worse, it has felt like ten!! Who just meets someone on a night out and decides to practically move in with them? Are you sure you were not held against your will? Is someone watching you? You can tell us."

I burst out laughing in unison with Jessica and Sophia whilst Whitney kept a straight face. Intense questioning was something suited to her skillset; it is the reason she would be an incredible lawyer. Her poker face was extraordinary.

"I understand it may seem a little strange, but I definitely was not held against my will. I promise you that!"

Whitney pushed her glasses up onto her head, rolled her eyes and prepared herself.

"So, what is she like?"

I poised myself for the onslaught of questions that were soon to come.

"She is nice, really nice, amazing in fact. She is just something else. Obviously, her looks drew me to her at first, but once I got to know her, it was like her looks were her least exciting aspect. She is kind, funny, driven, caring, family orientated, loyal. Like everything you would want someone to be."

I was gushing over Alex, as I had been since the moment I met her, and that was obvious to see by all three of my friends.

Whitney was unphased when she spoke next.

"Well, if I were not mistaken, I would think that our little Kacy is rather smitten."

She said light-heartedly. She would often give me a hard time, but she only ever wanted the best for me. I smiled shyly and looked down at the table, embarrassed. Whitney continued.

"What about this past week? Come on; we want all the details. What have you been up to?"

I opted for the summarised version.

"We went to the movies; we ate at Alex's bar a few times; I met some of her friends the second time we went there, which was nice. They seemed lovely. I also met her sister a couple of days ago who owns the bar with her; she also seems great. We went for a long drive one day. Stayed in and watched quite a few movies. It has been nice. I suppose just being in her company has been the best thing about it all."

Jessica squeezed my arm in excitement. The next question was one I anticipated.

"And the sex?"

Whitney smirked, intentionally wanting to see me squirm. She knew exactly how uncomfortable I was about to become. I was all for grilling my friends about their sex life, but it was not something I could freely discuss when it came to my own.

"You know I do not like talking about stuff like that."

She laughed before responding.

"Come on, Kace, these are critical details."

There was only one way the conversation would focus on something other than my sex life. There was no alternative.

"Okay fine, it was out of this world, and I am not just saying that. Literally, the best I have ever experienced."

Sophia chipped in suddenly.

"Are we talking like Nathan Andrews out of this world?"

Nathan Andrews was a boy that Sophia used to hook up with for almost a full year. She did not like him all that much, not enough to make him her boyfriend but apparently, what he achieved in the bedroom was like nothing she had ever experienced, and therefore she kept him around. We now judged every sexual encounter any of us had on a scale of 1 to Nathan Andrews.

"I would say Nathan x 10!!"

They all gasped in harmony. Humorous as always.

"No way? Well, now I want to know more." Screeched Whitney.

"It is hard to explain. Let's just say she knew exactly what she was doing. Like EXACTLY. I did not have to advise or support in any way like I previously have done, and it happens a lot more than once if you understand what I am saying."

I could feel all eyes on me; enormous smiles crept across each one of their faces one by one.

"Ahh, okay, now it all makes sense. I see why you didn't want to leave your little love nest all week."

Jessica grinned. That had not been the only reason for me not wanting to leave, but the sexual chemistry between us had played a significant part in my reluctancy to vacate her bed on a daily basis.

"Can we change the subject now?"

The conversation eventually turned to weekend plans and TV shows. I was off the hook.

A month passed by in the blink of an eye, I tried to stay at home, but the urge to spend time with Alex was overcoming. I spent most nights at Alex's apartment. We lay awake for hours talking about everything; there was no subject off-limits. We watched the sunset almost every night; it became my favourite part of our evening routine.

It all seemed to pass by in a blur. We did nothing of extreme significance yet everything of worth. The memories of lying with her, kissing her, merely being in her presence were memories that would forever be embedded in my soul.

After almost two weeks solid staying at Alex's apartment, I ventured home to see my mom for lunch, and she had warned me, *"You will get sick of each other, you know, it is always more exciting if you give each other time to miss one another, sweetheart."*

I could see the apprehensive look on her face, but also the hint of a smile suppressing in the corners of her mouth. I knew deep down she was content with seeing me so happy, but her parental instincts would always be at the forefront. My reply had been light-hearted, *"I have spent every day with you and Dad for the past 21 years of my life, and I am not sick of you yet."*

Some might say me and Alex were moving too fast; it did not feel that way to me. We were going at a pace that felt comfortable to us.

I had never been the type to spring full force into a relationship. They take time to develop and perfect; I was far from unrealistic in that sense. I would always be the first to question my friends if they were reckless; a discussion regarding marriage and kids after mere months was absurd to me. Granted, that is my opinion, but I believe you do not honestly know someone until you have been with them for a substantial period of time. Some may refer to it as the *'honeymoon'* period.

That being said, I was beginning to wonder if I was about to be hypocritical of my own beliefs—a living, breathing contradiction.

The summer was scorching that year, averaging 30 degrees

every single day. When university finally concluded, we had nothing to do but enjoy the weather. Alex asked me to take a trip down to Wilmington to explore the beaches; they were by far the best across the whole 300 miles of barrier island stretch. The landscape was magical; people drove hundreds of miles just to relax and enjoy the atmosphere. The seafood on offer was to die for and served in the local bars all day.

There was something about being in Wilmington or being anywhere on the coast for that matter; all the unique small towns had something to offer. They were all so wonderful in their own way. Alex's family used to have a beach house down on Wilmington's coast, between Carolina and Kure beaches, one of two that they owned, the other one was over in Oregon. Unfortunately, they had to sell up once her parents passed away as they could no longer afford to keep it. A tear came to her eye as she explained all about the memories she had of that place.

We stayed in a B&B on the coast, just for one night. It was our first trip away together. We were approaching five weeks of dating, neither of us had expressed our desires to be officially a couple, although it felt to me like we were.

We lay on the beach that night after dinner, the sun had set, and the stars were sparkling in the flawless night sky. The Met Office predicted a meteor shower, which thrilled us both. I had only ever seen one meteor shower, but I was so young.

"I spoke to my grandma earlier. She said she can't wait to meet you one day soon."

Alex's grandma was very important to her and Natalie; she was the only family they had left. Their grandfather had died a year earlier, so Grandma Rose was everything to Alex.

"I cannot wait to meet her too. She sounds so lovely. Is she okay?"

"Natalie went to the doctor's with her this morning because

she has lost her appetite and feels a bit weak lately, but she just thinks it is nothing. They are going to do a few checks when she goes back next week."

Alex was casual in her speech, but I knew it concerned her that Rose was ill. She had just surpassed her 75th birthday and Alex so often worried about how much longer she would have left with her.

"I am sure it is something of nothing. Did she say anything else?"

Alex smirked and shook her head; she was secretive.

"What are you smiling at? What else did she say?"

Alex chuckled to herself. I could not resist flicking some sand her way in pretend annoyance. She rolled away in hysterics and then held her hand up, pleading for no more sand to be thrown.

"Please, no more."

I swiftly reached for another handful, threatening to throw it once again.

"Okay, okay, put the sand down and I will tell you what she said."

It appeared I had uncovered Alex Dawson's kryptonite.

"In a nutshell, she said that I should stop being so soft and just ask you to be my girlfriend."

Alex settled back onto her elbows and looked towards the stars; a mischievous smile crept upon her lips. She glanced at me from the corner of her eye, waiting patiently for my response.

"So, what are you waiting for?"

Alex turned towards me and took my hands in hers.

"Miss Kacy Sullivan, will you do me the honour of officially being my girlfriend?"

Alex was the queen of eye contact. Her eyes never wavered from mine once. She was grinning from ear to ear, a deadly combination of the most piercing blue eyes and perfect teeth. How could I say no to the gorgeous specimen sat before me?

"Of course I will. I could not think of anything better."

Then she kissed me, suddenly my heart skipped a beat, and my stomach exploded with a flurry of butterflies. A tremor ran through my whole body as it did every single time we locked lips that way. It was an epic evening in more ways than one.

Sometimes you cannot explain what you see in a person. The thought of Alex brought so many physical attributes to mind as well as personality traits that most would be enviable of. Still, in all honesty, sometimes it is just the way they seem to take you to a place where no one else can. Although we had only been dating for a short period of time, she was captivating. I only saw her; everything else around me when I was in her presence was merely just surroundings, environment, background noise. We lounged together under the stars for a little while longer. Then I saw the first shooting star.

"Alex look, up there on the left, can you see that?"

The child within me stared in utter astonishment.

"That is incredible." Alex whispered.

What I witnessed that night was one of the world's most awe-inspiring events. I was instantly taken back to my childhood. I remembered my grandma always used to tell me, *"If you ever see a shooting star Kacy, you must make a wish. If it is something you want enough, then it will always come true."*

"Shall we make a wish?"

I suggested to Alex.

"Sure, you first."

There was no need to overthink my wish. The first thing that came to mind was exactly what I thought it would be. I wished for the feeling I had at that moment to never change.

"What did you wish for?"

I asked curiously. Alex looked amused.

"You know if I tell you they don't come true right? Did nobody ever tell you that?"

I was desperate to know what she had wished for and whether it resonated with mine.

"That is a myth. You have to tell me now; I am intrigued."

Alex sat up and pulled the extra blanket from her bag; the night was getting cooler. She reached out her arm and ushered me in, leisurely wrapping the blanket around the back of us both. After a moment like that, she told me her wish.

"I wished for you, Kacy."

"What do you mean, you wished for me?"

At first, she was reluctant to elaborate. I could only assume she didn't want to show her vulnerability.

"I wished that I would get many more moments like this with you. That we can make a million more memories like this one. I just wished for you, in every sense."

I was starting to fall for Alex Dawson, and how could I not? I no longer envied the kind of romance you saw in the movies because that was what we had. My life in that moment was as close to perfect as I felt it would ever be. I was a simple girl. I never wanted someone who would promise me the moon and the stars; that was unrealistic. When I searched myself, I merely wanted someone who would promise to lie beneath them with me. Alex was that someone for me.

As we lay there underneath the shooting stars, watching as each one shone brighter than the last, each making its way through the sky in a unique way. I thought about other people all over the world that would be wishing on those same stars. Would they be hoping for health? Or wealth? Or love? Or happiness? Everyone had a wish. A brief time passed before Alex spoke again.

"I remember sitting on our old porch at night with my grandma, it was not long after my parents passed and she told me something, she said that no matter where you are in the world you will always see the same stars so if you ever get lonely just look up at the sky and know that your parents are seeing those same stars, wherever they are now, they are watching them with you."

I could not imagine what it must have been like for her, losing both parents at the tender age of 21. Alex would often reference them in situations, and I would just listen and let her reminisce.

"I think your grandma is a very wise woman, and that is a beautiful thing to believe in Alex. Never let that go."

Grandparents almost always knew the right thing to say. It must be a combination of age and experience. They have experienced most things in life, made mistakes and learnt from them, so they always know what to say and how to make you feel better, even in your darkest hour.

"It might seem ridiculous, but I suppose it gives me some hope, thinking that they are still out there somewhere."

Grief was not something I was overly familiar with. All I could do was comfort her in that moment. The meteor shower continued for 30 minutes. As they became less frequent, we packed up our belongings and made our way back to the Bed & Breakfast.

The rest of the evening and the next day with Alex was picture-perfect; it could not have gone any better. We were officially a couple, and that made me happier than I had ever been.

CHAPTER FOUR

My final exam. The relief as I escaped the campus almost brought a tear to my eye. I felt confident, and there was nothing left to do other than eagerly await the results that would arrive roughly a month later. I would soon have a Bachelor's Degree in Architecture, and the prospect filled me with so much joy. I had found out a week earlier that I had an internship spot guaranteed at my dad's company, providing I passed my exams, which meant I could gain adequate job experience for a year, before I looked to take my Master's Degree. I had every faith in myself that I could do it. I had dedicated countless hours to the cause, practically living in the library and burying my head in books. I would not allow the final semester's exams to defeat me.

There had been a minor distraction in recent months, Alex Dawson to be precise, but she had supported me as much as she could, making sure I had ample time to study, she knew how important it was to me, and I adored her for that.

As I made my way towards the parking lot, I felt a tight squeeze from behind. I turned to see Alex looking as impeccable as ever with a large bunch of white roses in her hands. My favourite.

"Alex! What are you doing here?"

I threw my arms around her. It had only been 48 hours since I had seen her last, but it felt like a lifetime.

"Hi, gorgeous! I thought I would surprise you, maybe take you for some food if you fancy it?"

I beamed from ear to ear as she handed me the flowers.

"They are beautiful. Thank you! I would love to go for some lunch. I am starving."

I studied her as I often did. The gym attire worked in her favour, shorts, running trainers and an incredibly tight t-shirt that showed off just how athletically built she was. Her hair was pulled up into a bun off her face, a look that she did not don very often, but I loved it when she did.

"Here, let me take that bag. It looks heavy."

She removed the bag from my shoulder to her own then placed her arm around my waist, leading me towards the car. She kissed my forehead as she always did, and I felt the same sense of pride I had been feeling every day for almost two months.

"How did the exam go?"

She mumbled as she pulled her lips away from my forehead.

"Really well, I think. I felt pretty confident with most of it. I spoke to a few of the others when we were leaving, and they felt the same. I guess I will just wait and see now."

I smiled reluctantly, there was always a worry about being overconfident, but Alex instantly made me feel even more at ease.

"If anyone can do it, you can. You are probably the smartest person I know, so I have no doubt in your ability."

We approached her car, and she opened the door for me; chivalry did not stop with men.

"We will come back for your car later, Kace, okay?"

I nodded in agreement and slid into the passenger side. Alex drove a Chevrolet pick-up truck; the car was vintage but in amazing condition. It had been her dad's pride and joy. It was not at all what I pictured her driving when I first met her, but the sentimental value of the car meant more to her than any other car possibly could.

The familiar purr of the engine started with the turn of the ignition. Within seconds we were on route to a local diner unbeknownst to me. An afternoon spent eating and drinking with my favourite person, so simple yet so satisfying.

The weeks became a blur. Alex and I were utterly inseparable, and that was just the way we liked it. We both had our own lives, and Alex still had a business to run, so although my days and nights were freed up for the remainder of the summer, Alex's, unfortunately, were not. I kept myself busy most of the time; my friends and family were always happy to have me around. I took up yoga with my mom once a week on a Tuesday, I went for dinner with Savannah every Wednesday, and I saw Whitney almost every day. She was my best friend, after all, we had been best friends for so long that the pressure of arranging plans did not exist anymore. We would seldom turn up on one another's doorsteps and let ourselves in. Whether the other felt like the company or not, that was a real friendship.

Alex mainly worked day shifts at the bar, but some nights she had to work late, primarily to oversee the general running if Natalie or the other shift manager was not there. Natalie preferred to work the late shift; she had worked in bars since she was 18 years old, so she lived for the liveliness. That suited Alex just fine because she preferred the home environment.

If Alex found herself on a late shift, she would often finish at around 2 am depending on how busy the bar was. They rang the bell for last orders at 1 am, which is when most of the customers ventured into the nightclubs further uptown. I would often arrive at the bar around 1 am to keep Alex company whilst she locked up and put the money away. I was continually up at that time anyway. I could not seem to find a consistent sleeping pattern. The number of times I had turned in at 3 am and then been up for a class at 6 am was shocking. I am still surprised I made it through those days.

It was Friday 19th August, and for some reason unknown to me at the time, that night was unusual. The bar was already closed when I arrived just after midnight. I thought to myself that maybe she had shut up early, Friday nights were never as busy as Saturday's, but the lights were out, and as I peered through the window, it was vacant, not a single person inside.

Then it suddenly dawned on me; I had not received a text from Alex for almost four hours. Had it really been that long? I pondered. She always found the time to check-in, even when she was swamped. In my mind, there was only one logical explanation; she must have left early, but why? Why hadn't she told me? Where had she gone?

So many questions that I did not know how to get the answers to. I walked the five short minutes to her apartment. Maybe she had gone home, perhaps she had felt unwell, and her phone had died. That would be a reasonable excuse for her lack of communication.

Alex's apartment was empty when I arrived. I knew where the spare key was located, so I immediately let myself in. The apartment did not look out of place in any way; no foul play suspected. It was the same as it had been that morning when I left. Relief. I half expected to find Alex in bed, confirming my theory that she had come down with a sudden illness, but the bed was still perfectly made.

I pulled out my cell phone again, still no reply. I tried to call also, still no answer. At that point, I started to panic. There was a devastating feeling in the pit of my stomach; I felt utterly helpless. So many possibilities ran through my head.

Had she been abducted? Dramatic, I know.

Held at gunpoint for the weekends' takings? Possible.

Maybe she was at the police station. Also possible.

Hospital? Had she been involved in an accident? That did not bear thinking about.

Never once in the midst of my theatrical scenarios did it cross my mind that she may have been unfaithful. Women threw themselves at Alex on a daily basis. I had been present on two occasions when women had written their phone numbers on their receipts and handed them back when paying the bill. It was not bothersome to her; she found it flattering. At first, I grew incredibly jealous, but I soon realised that I trusted her more than anyone; maybe that was slightly naive for the length of time we had been together.

Over an hour of anguish and uncertainty passed. I was almost ready to phone 911 when my phone lit up; it was Alex calling.

"Alex!! Why have you not called? Are you okay? I have been going out of my mind."

There was silence on the line for a few seconds as she steadied herself to speak.

"I don't…I don't know how to say it…my grandma… has got…she has Cancer."

Her words almost a whisper as she forced herself to say the dreaded word.

"Oh god, Alex, I am so sorry. That is awful. Are you at the hospital now? I would have come with you."

My heart broke inside.

"Yes, I am. I should have called. I rushed straight to the hospital once Nat told me. I barely had time to think."

She sounded so exhausted and demoralised. My body yearned to be there to comfort her.

"Don't worry, I understand. I cannot imagine how this is affecting you. I wish I could help. Is Natalie still there with you?"

Her response was quick and pressured.

"She is yes. Sorry, Kace, I need to go, the doctor is here. I will call you later."

"Okay, let me know. Say hello to Rose and Natalie."

I barely had time to respond before the phone went dead. My heart sank into the pit of my stomach, she sounded so unbelievably heartbroken, and I was entirely helpless. I had only met Rose once, the week prior, and she had to be the most delightful person I had ever met, so kind, tentative, and worldly. She made me feel unbelievably welcome in her home. She had spent her whole life helping others, working with numerous charities whilst caring for her parents and later in life, she fostered children for close to 15 years. She was a selfless woman, and she did not deserve a disease so cruel to inhabit her body.

I received a text message just over an hour later from Alex.

They have said she has cancer of the stomach, and it has spread to most of her major organs; that is why she was struggling to eat. The weakness and the stomach pains it is all to do with the cancer. They basically said it is too late and there is nothing they can do. Not even a young fighting fit person would survive a cancer as fierce. They have predicted she could have anything from 1 to 3 months left to live. She is everything to me, Kacy. How do I begin to process that information? She is all me and Nat have left. We are going to take her home now and figure out the next steps.
I will call you tomorrow.
Goodnight.

I could not begin to imagine the pain Alex must have been feeling at that moment in time. She had already lost her grandfather a year prior and then her parents before that in such a tragic way, to now discover the devastating news about her grandma was the ultimate blow. I could do nothing to fix the situation, nothing I could do would make it any better for Alex or Rose. To sit by and watch someone you care so deeply for suffer was the most heart-breaking of experiences. I climbed into Alex's bed with a heavy heart and gradually fell to sleep.

The morning arrived abruptly. It was 11 am, and I woke to a text from Alex explaining that she was on route back home. I was relieved; I needed to see her and comfort her in any way I could.

Alex arrived back at her apartment at noon. Her face was so drawn; the sadness in her voice when she spoke and the lack of energy she now possessed was upsetting. Alex was always so cheerful, happy, energetic, and that was what I adored about her. I had never seen her any other way. She threw her keys and phone on the black, vintage side table to her left as she entered. She walked immediately over to the breakfast bar and slumped into the nearest chair. I embraced her tightly.

"Hey, babe. How are you feeling?"

I didn't know what to say; there are no perfect words in that situation. I was unsure if she wanted me there at all; I could not read her in that moment.

"Not great, as good as I can be, I guess. Thank you for being here; it means a lot."

She stood as I relaxed my embrace, turning to kiss me on the forehead. She then kicked off her shoes and advanced to the sofa.

"I wanted to be here for when you got back. How is Rose?"

I smiled sympathetically.

"She took the news surprisingly better than me and Natalie did. When we got her home, she told us she had already prepared herself for the worst, so it wasn't a shock."

I wanted her to open up to me. She knew she could tell me anything, but on the other hand, I completely understood that it was difficult for her to come to terms with it all.

"They say that we know our bodies better than the doctors. I admire her for being so strong. Is Natalie with her now?"

"Yes, she keeps insisting she is okay, but I will not take the risk of leaving her alone."

Alex hunched over on the edge of the sofa, a far cry from the woman I saw 24 hours earlier.

"I understand that. When will you head back to see her? Would you like me to come with you?"

"I said I would head back in the morning. I needed to come home and speak to you first."

She placed her head in her hands and sighed before she continued. I was suddenly concerned for what was about to come next. She looked distressed, vacant almost. When she raised her head and looked my way, my heart sank.

"I have to go away for a while, Kace."

"What do you mean?"

My response was barely audible.

"My grandma only has months left, and that is if we are lucky. She cannot spend them here, just waiting to die. She wants to be at her favourite place, down on the coast of Oregon, a place called Cannon Beach. She and my granddad used to go there several times a year; she hoped they would move there together one day. We discussed it at length this morning, and that is where she wants to spend her last days."

She paused for a split second, composing herself in the best way she could.

"I have to give her that wish, Kacy. Me and Natalie both

agreed we need to do this for her. She would not want us to put our lives on hold, but we owe her that. She has always been there for us, through everything, and now this is her time of need."

The tears welled in Alex's eyes, those beautiful blue eyes. I saw the agony within them. She took my hands in hers and looked without deviation at me for reassurance. I tried not to cry; it was not about me, I told myself repeatedly in my head. She could see I had no response imminently, so she continued.

"I am sorry. I guess that makes things difficult for us. I just can't think about that right now, my head is pounding, and I have no idea what to do. I feel like I am about to relive my parent's death all over again."

I repositioned myself beside her, holding her in my arms as she sobbed. I felt guilty for thinking of myself, allowing the thoughts of what it meant for our relationship to consume me. At that moment, the fact that Alex was soon to lose her beloved grandma had to be the only important thing. I certainly did not resent her for that; she would always do the right thing by her family, just as anyone should. My response was one of limited value and it croaked from my lips.

"I understand. I am so sorry you are going through this. Just know that I will support you as best I can through everything."

She looked up at my tear sodden face.

"Kace, will you lie with me for a few hours, please?"

It felt like a plea. As if she would ever need to question what my answer would be.

"Of course, I will. Anything you need."

On reflection, I should have said more. I should have told her that everything would be okay, that it was okay for her to give Rose her last wish, that she need not worry about what that meant for us because we would find our way back to each other. I should have said a lot more than what I did, and if I could go back, I would have, but I was truly speechless in that moment. Why did I lie there, holding her and thinking that it was always too good to be true? The selfishness within me wanted to wallow in self-pity. She was about to lose the most important person in her life, and that was a grand catastrophe that I knew absolutely nothing about.

We lay like that together, entwined into one another for what felt like a lifetime. Neither of us said anything, but the silence spoke a thousand words.

Eventually, Alex retreated to her bedroom and began to pack her things. I silently folded her clothes and aided her in packing most of her belongings into two large suitcases. We made eye contact every so often, and all either of us could muster was a sorrowful smile.

"Have you thought about who will run the bar? I assume you will need to hire some help. I can always pick up some shifts if you are struggling. You know I will help in any way I can."

She perched on the edge of the bed.

"We have someone who works for us that can pick up the managerial side of things. The bar staff we have are great, and I know they will pick up extra shifts and do everything they can to keep things running smoothly whilst we are away. Thank you for offering though Kace, it means a lot."

I wanted her to know above everything else that I would be there for her in whatever capacity she needed.

"Where will you stay in Cannon Beach?"

She shrugged, evidently unsure what her plans would be at that precise moment.

"We are going to look into it over the next few days. We need to look at what is the most cost-effective way to start with. There is my grandma's house to think about, as well as her belongings, her car. She insists we sell it all to fund our stay in Cannon Beach, but as you can imagine, it is just a lot to process all at once. We just don't have the time to wait for stuff like that before we go, so it will need to take a back seat."

It must be so difficult knowing you only have a limited amount of time left with someone you love. At that point, all the material things like houses and cars become so irrelevant. It is sad that it takes the inevitable idea of death for many of us to realise that love, health, and happiness are the most important things in the world.

"I feel like this is all happening so fast. I am going to miss you so much Alex."

I understood that every moment for her was precious, but it did not make the circumstances any easier. She gestured for me to sit down on the bed beside her.

"I am going to miss you so much too, Kace. I would ask you to come with us, but I know that is unrealistic. I know we have not known each other long enough to ask you to move five hours away from everything you know for god knows how long."

She was right; it wasn't logical. My parents would think it was unwise. My life was in Raleigh. I had my career to think about, and as much as I would miss Alex, ultimately, I felt like it was something she had to do on her own.

"I think we both know that this is something you need to do for yourself, but for what it is worth, I would move halfway around the world for you if it was required, regardless of how short-lived our relationship has been."

The realisation that my feelings for Alex had become even more profound hit me hard. I had genuinely fallen for her, and that was now a terrifying prospect.

"For what it is worth, I would move halfway around the world for you too."

Alex lifted my chin and pressed her lips faintly against

mine. There was a tenderness about the embrace, our lips had met in that way almost every day for the past two months, but that kiss was different. There was a desperation about the embrace, knowing that it may have been one of our last for a considerable period of time.

"Alex, do you think we can get through this? If you wanted to take a break, I would understand. I have never had a long-distance relationship. I doubt it is easy, and the last thing I want is to bring more pressure or stress to your current situation."

She shook her head, ferociously. My tension eased.

"What would bring me more stress would be knowing that I did not have you to come back home too. It will not be easy, but I believe what we have is worth it; you are worth it, so I know we can get through this together."

I knew what we had was special, something worth fighting for.

"Shall we try and somewhat enjoy our last night together? I would like to just lie here with you, eat lots of chocolate, watch some awful films and pretend our world is not about to completely change tomorrow. How does that sound?"

Alex nodded in agreement. I had no doubt her mind would be elsewhere, but her body was with me, and I would cherish the hours I had left to hold her.

"That sounds perfect."

The next day, we said goodbye. Alex Dawson had materialised into everything I had ever wanted; she was stood before me in all her glory, and I had no choice but to wave goodbye. The woman I had become utterly besotted with was now moving across the country and out of reach. Oregon was not across the country as such, but it was roughly five hours away by plane, which to me felt like the other side of the world.

I would soon be starting my career as an intern, and

architecture was not a straight forward Monday-Friday job. I would undoubtedly be doing long hours whilst I learnt the ropes and tried to prove myself worthy of such a role. The fact my father also worked at the firm brought added pressure. I knew there would be whispers of favouritism, so I would be on a mission to prove my worth from the beginning.

Taking everything into account, I knew I would have no time to make a 10 hour round trip to Oregon. It would not be forever, I told myself. I hoped for Alex's sake that it was longer than the doctors had predicted. Putting my emotional state aside, I hoped with all my heart that Rose would defy the odds for as long as possible.

The thought of not having Alex in my life every day broke my heart, but we could talk on the phone; modern technology meant keeping in touch was more straightforward than ever. So together, we vowed to make long-distance work; we had no choice. The other alternative was simply not acceptable.

Alex put the last of her belongings in the trunk of her pick-up and turned to face me. She leant against the passenger door and pulled me towards her for our final embrace. I had remained strong throughout that morning, and you could say optimistic about our future, but as I hugged her for the last time, the tears began to form.

"I am going to miss you so much, Kace. You have no idea. I will call you and text you every day. I promise we will get through this."

I embedded myself into her neck as I often did. Alex stood 2 inches taller than my 5'5" frame, the perfect height. I did not want to let go. Alex placed her hands on either side of my face and kissed me once on both cheeks, my forehead, nose and then my lips. A sudden rush of emotion engulfed my body. I could not let her leave without telling her how I felt.

"Alex…"

"Kacy…"

We spoke each other's name simultaneously, eager to tell the other what we were both feeling deep inside. The look in her eyes mirrored my own. There was almost no need for the words that would follow.

"I have fallen in love with you, Alex. I know it has only been a short time. I know that there is so much that needs to be worked out, but I want to be with you, no matter what."

Rejection had never crossed my mind. She had to feel the same.

"I am so in love with you too. Honestly, meeting you that night was the best night of my life. I know we are only just beginning, and there is so much more in store for us."

The sincerity in her voice was heartfelt. I could not contain the smile on my face. The perfect woman who stood before me felt precisely the same way that I did.

"I really hope so."

I tried my hardest to fight back the tears.

"What time do you fly out again?"

It was just the start for us, and I knew when she returned to Raleigh, as heartbroken as she would be, we could work through it together. I would be there for her; I promised her that.

"6 pm tonight. Nat has just text saying she has found a suitable B&B for a few nights until we figure out more permanent accommodation."

She pulled me in close to her once again. Alex had always made me feel so safe and protected in her arms; I craved that.

"Will you call me before you fly and when you land?"

She smiled softly.

"Of course I will."

We spent a minute in the same embrace. I savoured every taste of her lips on mine before it was finally time for her to leave. I stood by the sidewalk, waving farewell to the woman I loved as she drove off into the distance, wondering how soon I would see her again.

I had truly fallen in love with Alex Dawson. I had fallen in love with her heart, her soul, and her body. The courage she possessed, the confidence that shone through her, and the overwhelming kindness evident to anyone who knew her. Just a few quality's taken from a long, ever-growing list that made her who she was.

Despite my world being upside down, I told myself that I would always love her, even if she turned out to be someone else or the world painted a picture of her that should not be. I would still love her; I knew it then, and I would know it always.

CHAPTER FIVE

"Good evening, beautiful."

The familiar voice brought instant joy to my excruciatingly stressful day.

"Alex, I have missed your voice."

It had been a mere 24 hours since our last phone conversation, but it felt like an eternity.

"Not as much as I have missed yours. You think it would get a little easier, huh?"

It had not, quite the opposite. With each day that passed, I yearned to see her more.

"You would think! How is Grandma Rose today?"

It was always without fail the first question I asked. Alex kept me regularly informed, I knew there would be minor changes, if any, but it was polite to ask.

"She is doing great. We went to the doctor's today. She has officially surpassed the two-month mark. The doctor thinks she could have another two months if things continue to develop at the rate they are doing, but they keep warning us that things can change overnight."

I could sense the warranted enthusiasm in her voice.

"That is amazing news Alex. I bet you are so happy."

The news pleased me, above all else.

"I had no doubt in my mind that she would fight; she is a wonder is our Rose. It makes me so happy that every day I get to wake up and see her smile. It is the greatest feeling in the world, knowing she is somewhere she loves, a place full of memories."

I could tell Alex was beaming from ear to ear. She had made the right decision by Rose and not once had she regretted it. That alone warmed my heart.

"She certainly is, and I hope so much that she continues to defy the odds. I checked in on the bar for you tonight, like you asked."

On several occasions, Alex had asked me to pop my head in, go for a few drinks with the girls, a spot of lunch with my mom, etc. That way, it would not seem like I was spying on them in any way, but I guess you could say for all intensive purposes I was.

"Thank you. I take it everything was okay? I spoke with Johnny yesterday and all seemed well, but I worry they are hiding things from me sometimes. I know they would be wary of causing me extra stress if anything was to go wrong."

Johnny was the new bar manager whilst Alex and Natalie remained out of town. He had worked for them for four years and was more than qualified from his previous bar manager job roles; he seemed like the ideal fit. I watched him eagerly every time I went in, he knew who I was, and he did not so much as bat an eyelid. From what I could see, Johnny was an outstanding professional, and I always had nothing but positive feedback for Alex.

"Everything was excellent. It was as bustling as ever. The place has not burnt down; there were no bar brawls or disgruntled customers. It was running as smoothly as ever; almost smoother, I think, than when you ran it. Maybe you should keep Johnny on, and then you can have all the time in the world to spend with me."

I teased; humour had been a tough emotion to evoke in Alex of late. We would find ourselves laughing and joking, trying to find some normality in our situation, but I knew afterwards she would feel guilty that the life we hoped and dreamed for us both would not involve Rose.

"Maybe I will do that. I can be at your every disposal then, which I am sure you would enjoy. I cannot believe it has been two whole months since I saw your beautiful face."

The thought of her returning to Raleigh brought her great sorrow. As much as she yearned to see me, and vice versa, we knew that returning would mean only one thing. The two months had been difficult but not torment. Amazingly they had gone relatively quick. My long hours at work meant I had little time to think or do anything else; it was a welcome distraction.

"I know, it has gone relatively quick though, surprisingly. That reminds me I have a suggestion."

It was something I had been contemplating for a few days prior.

"A suggestion? I am all ears."

I cut straight to the chase.

"Well, I can take some time off work soon. We are coming to the end of a couple of big contracts, and they have said now would be the ideal time to take a few days off. So, I was thinking, in a couple of weeks, I could fly to Oregon. If that were something that suited you of course, it would only be for the weekend, but I would love to see you and Rose."

I was cautious in my approach. She expressed the desire to see me on a daily basis, but I also knew her time was occupied, and I did not want to interfere in any way.

"I would love that! That sounds like a perfect idea Kace. Let me run it by Rose first, check she is okay for us to have someone else here for a few days. I am sure she would love the idea though; you are all I talk about apparently so, maybe she would like you to be here in the flesh to avoid having the same conversation with me for the 60th day in a row."

The fact she spoke about me regularly filled me with such a sense of belonging.

"Perfect, just let me know then, and we can get it arranged. I love that you talk about me, by the way; that makes me feel good."

I gushed.

"Of course, I do, every day. It has been unbelievably hard not being able to see you. I know I have told you this before, but I cannot risk not being here if something happened. I would never forgive myself and I know you understand that."

I did understand it completely. Alex coming back to Raleigh, even for a weekend, was justifiably not an option.

"Well, just so you know, I talk about you all the time too. All my friends have just about had enough of my continuous pining, as they like to put it. I on the other hand, can only assume they are jealous."

We laughed effortlessly as we always did.

"How was work today? I had a look at the plan you sent over; it looks amazing. I know nothing about architecture, but I appreciate you sharing it with me. It is always nice to see your world."

Every day invariably, she would ask about work. I was unsure if she genuinely wanted to hear it or just asked as part of her good-mannered nature. I would often bore her by talking about new construction projects and redevelopments. Everything from the budget to sustainability. She would listen and ask questions as if it interested her greatly. I adored her for that.

"Work was long. I managed to get away at five today, though. There are still a few adjustments to make to the plan I sent you, but most of it has been agreed upon. I worked so hard on that with my dad. Last night after I spoke to you, we stayed up until midnight in his study working on it. I am starting to forget my life before Architecture."

I was lucky to have such a great mentor and teacher in my own home.

"It must be nice to share the same passion as your dad. I am proud of you for following your dreams. Plus, I like the sound of my girlfriend being a big-time Architect. We know who will pay for everything."

Alex joked.

"Says the one who owns her own business, maybe one day you can expand, and I can live out the rest of my days as a housewife."

I liked the sound of that.

"It seems we have a lot to iron out. It is a good job we have the rest of our lives."

The thought of our future together brought uncontainable excitement.

"Do you have any plans tomorrow?"

Our conversations always flowed the same way, but they never became monotonous. I loved knowing her plans, even insignificant details.

"Tomorrow, no, I don't believe so. We will probably read some Jane Austin on the porch and watch the world go by. Go for a stroll, afternoon tea, the usual. On Saturday though me and Nat are taking Rose into town. There is a carnival on; it's an annual thing, so that should be fun."

After a week of being in Cannon Beach, they settled on a charming little house by the beach with a vast back porch that overlooked the sea. There were four emerald green rocking chairs that the owners had recently upcycled. These chairs were now the perfect place for Alex, Natalie, and Rose to sit and reminisce as she had wished.

"I love carnivals so much. I have not been to one in years. I am so jealous! You will have a great time."

"Rose is excited because she remembers going there with my grandpa over 20 years ago. It is just another chance I can give her to remember the good times. I worry about taking her out too much; her immune system is a lot weaker than it used to be. I don't want to open her up to any type of virus, but she is stubborn, and she insists on going."

How bittersweet.

"Your aim is to make her happy, so let her do as she pleases. From what I know of Rose, she will do what she wants regardless, won't she."

Alex laughed.

"She has always been the same; she never would listen to a word my grandpa said, or my parents for that matter. Did I tell you when she took me out of 5th grade for two weeks because she found an excellent deal on a trip to Mexico? Her words to my mom were, *'what do they learn in 5th grade anyway, I will teach them about Mexico's history instead'* She's always been a law unto herself, but in a great way."

We spoke for an hour like that before my dad knocked on my bedroom door and summoned me to the study.

"Babe, I am going to go. If I want to have any chance of seeing you soon, I need to make sure I get these projects finished. The quicker they are done, the quicker I can kiss that face I miss so very much."

She spoke in her *'cute'* voice as she called it for the next part.

"I love you. I will call you tomorrow."

"I love you more, Alex Dawson. Sweet dreams."

The following day came rapidly, the lack of sleep was starting to take its toll, but it was nothing that a large coffee would not fix. I woke up to a string of text messages from Alex. One wished me a wonderful day, followed by a picture of her walking along the beach, followed by a picture of a large cup of coffee. She too, must have had a rough night's sleep.

Alex was often awake before me. Rose was an early bird and loved to watch the sunrise on her morning stroll along the beach, something Alex grew to love over the time she spent there. I received a picture every morning of the sunrise; it made me wish I could be there with her even more.

The first two months apart had been difficult, but I found solace in my work whilst Alex threw herself into her new role. I had already been noticed by several board members, which for an intern, was unheard of. Making a good impression was at the forefront of my mind, so to see it manifesting before me was a relief.

On further inspection of the sunrise photo, I could see Rose off to the left of the shot taking in the beauty of what was before her. I was so relieved for Alex; I know she was grateful for every second she got to spend with Rose. All I could hope was that when the day came, she would be able to find peace in the late memories she had created.

The conversation the night before made me so appreciative. I was filled with the confidence that nothing had changed between us. Throughout the first month Alex was away, I struggled to be content with our situation. You never know how much a relationship can endure when it becomes long distance. I am not afraid to admit that a thousand different scenarios went through my mind as our story started to unravel.

What would we become? When I thought about mine and Alex's story, it brought me the most joy to know that the best part was yet to come. It was not a story about me or about her, but about us, as a collective. Alex had become such a massive part of my life; the memories we had already created and the ever-growing feelings we shared brought with it a euphoria greater than anything else.

My heart sank the moment I realised just how much I wanted her, how much I needed her. She moved me in a way that was breathtaking to me, in a way that made every other woman on the planet seem so pale and incomparable beside her. I pulled myself from the trance that had captivated me and quickly prepared myself for another long day at work. I was officially on the countdown to a potential meeting with the woman I loved, and that was all the motivation I needed.

I arrived home at 7 pm. The greeting from my mother was a welcome one.

"Hi, Darling! Come here; I am ordering in for dinner. Would you like anything?"

It was Friday night, the weekend had arrived and with it came two long-overdue mornings in bed, a much-needed catch up with my best friends, a takeaway, and potentially some drinks on the town.

"Hi, Mom, I would love something! Where are you ordering from?"

I entered the kitchen with a spring in my step.

"I think the boys want Pizza, so probably Pizza Guru."

My favourite takeaway.

"Sounds perfect, pepperoni for me please."

I kissed her on the cheek and headed for the stairs. Friday night was family night, a tradition I adored. Food would typically take an hour which meant I had time to speak to Alex and find out how her day had been. Other than a quick text on my short-lived lunch, I had not spoken a word to her. The dial tone was promptly interrupted by the voice I missed so much.

"Kace, my beautiful girl."

The excitement in her voice was just as genuine as my own. That made me smile.

"Hello, you."

We quickly began to ramble on as we always did, every detail of our daily lives examined, leaving no stone unturned.

"I met an old friend today. Did I ever tell you about a girl called Jennifer?"

Initially, I thought absolutely nothing of her referencing another girl's name.

"No, I don't think you have. Who is she?"

I was genuinely curious.

"Her name is Jennifer Locksley. I may have mentioned one of my grandma's old friend's called Ms Locksley. She is her granddaughter."

I did not recall a Ms Locksley, but then again, I suppose there was a lot I was yet to discover about Alex's childhood. I allowed her to continue.

"We basically grew up together down here, me, Nat, Jennifer, and her sister Charlotte. Whenever we would come for the summer, we were inseparable."

There was a pang of jealousy creeping in the more Alex spoke.

"That must have been nice. When was the last time you saw her?"

I did not want to appear overly eager to know the details, so I kept the questions to a minimum.

"Probably nine years ago. We stopped going on vacation there when I was about 14 or 15, if I remember correctly. We tried to stay connected after that, but this was 2002/2003, so it was a bit more difficult then."

I wonder what she looked like being the overriding thought in my mind.

"Wow, so how did you bump into each other today? Does she live in Cannon Beach, or did she just vacation there as well?"

The conversation made me uneasy; the two months apart heightened certain emotions. Alex continued.

"She has lived here all her life. She now owns a little café that her family used to run. Her parents handed the keys over to her about three years ago. Funnily enough, we went to the café for some lunch, and she recognised us straight away. We got talking, and it was just nice to catch up. Ms Locksley is still in the area, so Rose is hoping to have a catch up with her soon."

Alex paused, awaiting my response.

"What a coincidence, that must have been nice, and I'm sure it will be lovely for Rose to see an old friend again."

"Absolutely, I think they are going to meet us at the carnival tomorrow. I really wish you could be here."

Me too, so it could be made abundantly clear that you have a girlfriend, I thought inaudibly to myself.

"I wish I could be there too."

Thank god for social media; I would soon be delving into the world of Jennifer Locksley. An hour passed and my mom called out that it was time to eat.

"Sorry Alex, I need to go, food has arrived. Text me later before you go to sleep though, okay?"

I knew she would, whether I reminded her or not.

"Okay. Enjoy your food and your evening. I love you."

"I love you too."

There were still things I wanted to ask. The rest of the conversation about both of our days had left my mind entirely, leaving it fixated only on Jennifer. Who was she? What did she look like? How did she dress? Was she cooler than me? Did she have a boyfriend or a girlfriend? Who is to say she was even gay? By the time I had done obsessing, I was jumping to conclusions that were far-fetched and ridiculous. None the less I at least had to know who she was because that's what any normal person would do, right?

That night the investigating commenced.

CHAPTER SIX

Saturday's for me consisted of movies, coffee, and a visit from Whitney. Work had become so exhausting that my weekends had become incredibly uninspiring. The weekend of the carnival was no different.

My detective abilities the night before had uncovered some details about Jennifer Locksley. She was 26 years old and single, according to her social media. She was pretty, much to my dismay, really pretty in fact. Her photos looked so effortless, a casual laugh here or a candid glance there. The wavy brunette hair she donned sat just below her shoulders, she wore it down in all her pictures, and it suited her. She was slim but curvy, pale-skinned considering she lived by the beach, and she had lips to envy.

Upon further investigation, it was apparent she was not one to post much of her life. The last post had been four months prior, a picture of her and someone called Olivia. They looked cosy in the picture, but I could not tell if there was anything more than friends. After an hour of snooping, I gave in, realising at that stage, my efforts were somewhat unjustified.

It was 3 pm, and like the hurricane she was, in came Whitney, bounding through my bedroom door like she owned the place.

"How is my best friend this fine Saturday afternoon?"

She was in a delightful mood, which meant one of two things, either she had found a new male friend to keep her company, or she wanted something, I suspected the latter.

"Tired. Who let you in?"

I rolled over in my bed and pulled the covers up high; she was radiating too much enthusiasm for me to contend with.

"Well, thank you for the welcome greeting! I have missed you too! You do realise I still have a key to your house that I never gave back?"

That is where my spare key went.

"So, you are the key stealer."

I should have known.

"I figured it would benefit everyone involved for me to just hold onto it a little longer. Remember that time I had to wake Michelle and George up after midnight? I assume they don't want that again."

I remember, alright, how annoyed they were the following day when I got the cold shoulder over breakfast.

"You mean the time that you decided you just had to have the '*cute nude*' bag for your date the next day, and It could not wait until a normal hour? I am sure my parents loved you for that."

In fact, their exact words did not emit love at all.

"I was passing through the neighbourhood; it seemed like a clever idea at the time. Anyway, enough of that, I have a key, and I am not giving it back. Swiftly moving on, how are my favourite star-crossed long-distance lovers?"

She was stalling, It would only be a matter of time until she revealed the real reason she had come, but I played along anyway.

"I am assuming you are referring to Alex and me and not Romeo and Juliet? We are good, same as the last time you asked; you know how it is. I miss her. I wish I could see her. I miss her some more. It's kind of repetitive."

I considered mentioning Jennifer, but what was there to discuss really? I was being paranoid; I knew that, so I chose to bury my late-night shenanigans as if it never happened.

"It is repetitive, a bit like your life lately. Which is why…"

Here we go, I thought.

"We should go on a night out…tonight."

The prospect filled me with dread. I mean, what would I even wear.

"Don't even say *'what do I wear'* you have a wardrobe full of clothes that still have tags on."

How did she always know exactly what I was thinking? She counteracted every thought I had before I even had the chance to express it. Weird.

"And do not say you are too tired. You have been lying in bed all day, so that is impossible. Do you want to know what I have done today?"

I knew better than to answer those rhetorical questions.

"I have been on a 10k run, picked up my dry cleaning, cleaned my car, met a boy for coffee and spent an hour at the mall doing some retail therapy hoping that I can persuade my best friend to come out tonight."

Whitney yanked the cover down so my whole face was exposed, leaving me with no choice but to witness her *'feel sorry for me'* look. She dashed over to the door and retreated with one of three bags she had unloaded on her way in.

"Did you need to pull the sheet off? I understand that your day has been very productive, and I am proud of you for that, but just for today, my productiveness reaches as far as the bedside table where I often reach for the remote so I can change the channel."

She rolled her eyes and handed me a plain black paper bag.

There was no indication from the packaging that would give me any hints about what was inside.

"Open it." She squealed.

I propped myself up, suddenly intrigued by the package before me.

"What is it?"

I peered inside the bag and pulled out a beautifully bound leather journal with a quote on the front that read, *'If someone buys you a journal as nice as this one, then you should really do anything they ask'* I immediately burst out laughing.

"Seriously? These are the lengths you're going to now to persuade me to go on a night out?"

In all seriousness, the journal was stunning and much needed.

"No, that quote just happens to fit in with our current circumstances. I 100% did not ask the guy behind the counter to print that, and it was 100%, not $1 per word, which is absolutely scandalous."

She was unbelievable.

"You did not spend $1 per word? Honestly, Whitney Sawyer, you are insane. Can I just say though, for the record, it is gorgeous, so thank you very much."

I turned the pages, feeling the quality of each one. It was perfectly finished, the leather was of high-quality. The price tag would have been a hefty one.

"I know you needed a new one. You have only mentioned it about ten times in the past two months. So, there you go."

Whitney was good to me. As aggravating as she was sometimes, there was nobody quite like her. She used her ability of knowing me better than anyone else to her advantage. Clever.

"Okay, maybe I can be persuaded to go out tonight."

Whitney clambered her way onto the bed and squeezed me

firmly. She knew how to get her own way. If there were a class on that, she would graduate at the top.

"That is all I needed. I will love you and leave you. I have a million other things to do before I can even think about what to wear. Call me later?"

"I will."

The whirlwind that was Whitney Sawyer had left me with a journal in one hand and not the faintest idea of what had just happened. It was time to haul myself out of bed and seize the day. I showered, ate a late lunch, cleaned my room, and finished some work before continuing straight for my wardrobe to find something suitable for the evening's events.

I noticed the time tick slowly past 6 pm. Alex must have been home from the carnival by now, I concluded. I found my phone and hit dial.

"Alex…Alex…can you hear me?"

"Hi Kace, I can hear you, babe."

The response was muffled.

"Oh good. How was your day at the carnival?"

There was a delayed pause on the line before she answered. The signal was terrible. I could hear a faint sound of music and laughing in the background; it made it hard to concentrate on what she said next.

"It has been great. Rose has had so much fun. Watching the parade was her favourite part. I don't think I have ever seen her laugh so much; it completely warmed my heart. She ended up telling me so many stories about my grandpa and my parents. I could see her reliving it all; it was so sweet. I will tell you all about it someday."

The delight in her voice evident. It was clear to see just how happy that made her, which in turn made me happy. All Alex wanted was for Rose to enjoy every day she had left, and Alex did everything in her power to ensure that.

"That is great, Al. I am so happy for you, and I can't wait to hear all about the stories...can you hear me...what is all that noise in the background? I can hardly hear you."

The combination of piercing music turned all the way up, and hundreds of people gathering did not make the ideal background for a phone conversation.

"Sorry, Kace, I didn't realise it was so loud. I am back in town at the carnival; there is an after-party that goes on into the evening. Rose insisted I come back once I took her home. She claims she wants to see me have some fun, and at 23, I should not be going to bed every night at the same time as her."

She laughed to herself. To be fair, Rose did have a point. She must have been very persuasive to get Alex to leave her side for the evening.

"I don't blame you. It sounds fun there. I wish I could be with you! Is Natalie there too?"

I tried to sound upbeat. After all, she deserved to let her hair down. I could not help the pang of jealousy, knowing she was having fun without me, and I was not there by her side to share the experience. Once Alex left, I had struggled to have fun without her, I told myself that it was work-related, that I physically did not have time to have fun, but the truth was it just wasn't the same. I would find myself constantly thinking about her, just wishing I were home so I could talk to her on the phone. The absence of her affected me intensely.

"No, babe, Natalie is at home with Rose. I didn't feel comfortable with nobody being there, so she offered to stay. I told her to ring me if she needed anything at all."

So, who was she with?

"Oh, so you just went back to the carnival on your own?"

Alex's reply was nonchalant as expected.

"God, no. The old friend I told you about, Jennifer? Well, she is here too and a group of her friends, so I have some company. I really wish you were here!"

Instantly I felt uncomfortable. I could hear someone calling her name in the background. Was that Jennifer? The sudden rush of jealousy that had developed the night before returned.

"Do you need to go? It sounds like you are in demand."

Alex bellowed to some unknown person that she would be two minutes. Our conversation was about to be cut short.

"Sorry, Kace. They want to get some food. I will have to go; I don't want to seem rude."

There was no satisfaction for me with how the conversation would end, but it was not the time to pry. It was the first time she had been out and done something for herself in two months. I would not allow my caution to spoil that for her.

"Okay, but I haven't had my fix of you tonight. How on earth will I get to sleep?"

Light-hearted sarcasm was often my go-to when I felt uncomfortable. It made Alex laugh, and that instantly put me at ease.

"Is that a hint of sarcasm I detect, Kacy Sullivan? Just so you know, I never have my fix of you, even when we talk for hours. I promise I will make up for it tomor…"

The phone line abruptly went dead.

I tried to call back twice, no answer. Her phone's battery life left me without a goodbye. Sending a text would be pointless, but I felt the need to wish her a good evening whether she would receive it or not.

Suddenly the prospect of going on a night out was even less appealing. The guilt of letting Whitney down would far outweigh my disappointment of being left wanting more when it came to Alex, but there was an intuition I struggled to shake.

After contemplating the most effective way to subtly hint that I may cancel, I composed a message and hit send. Luckily for me, Whitney was quick to inform me that Savannah and

Jessica had already RSVP'd. I was familiar with Whitney Sawyer's mind; her aim by name dropping was to make me want to go even more. It was always a great night out when the four of us got together; she knew that, but her plan backfired because all it did was lessen the guilt.

My night was a restless one. I checked my phone every five minutes. I scrolled through social media, hoping there would be some sign of her so I could at least take comfort in knowing her whereabouts. The time got to 11 pm, still nothing, no word from Alex. My eyelids felt heavy, drained, and just all together exhausted. The time had come to call it a night.

I picked up my phone one last time; within seconds, I had composed a goodnight message. I could not lay emphasis on what Alex may or may not be doing anymore. It was finally time to sleep.

When I spoke to Alex the next day, our conversation was brief, but it clarified my assumption from the night before.

"I am so sorry about last night, Kace. My phone died."

"I thought that might be the case. I was hoping you'd have called me when you got home, but I was exhausted. I couldn't stay awake past 11."

Why had she stayed out so late? My curiosity at an all-time high.

"I know I was out later than I expected. I got in around midnight. I wanted to come home earlier once my phone died, I felt bad that I couldn't speak to you, but you know what it's like. I didn't want to be the spoilsport."

My gut told me to ask questions, pry a little more into the going's on at the Carnival, but my heart did not want an answer that would potentially plant any more seeds of doubt.

"Well, I am glad you had a wonderful time anyway. Try not to let your phone die today; I missed you."

She chuckled.

"It never dies, but I spent all day taking photos of Nat and Rose. I got an entertaining video of us all on the Ferris Wheel. I will send them over after we get off the phone."

The conversation came hurriedly to a close after 20 minutes. I awaited the photos of Alex, something to look forward too on an otherwise gloomy Sunday. Our conversation had been slow, my mind toying persistently with what I should and shouldn't say.

I would often give my friends good advice when it came to relationships, but accepting my own advice seemed more difficult than it ought to be. The familiar cliché's like *'you have to trust until you are given a reason not to'* or *'communication is the key to a healthy relationship'* both absolutely true. The latter I struggled with. On several occasions, I wanted to speak to Alex about my insecurities, but the words deserted me.

Did I even have any real cause to be concerned? My mind would flashback to my first girlfriend and her parting comment, *'nobody wants a jealous and insecure girl Kacy, it's not a desired trait'* funnily enough, that was just before I found out she had been unfaithful. I would bite my tongue for the foreseeable.

The next day arrived in a heartbeat. Mondays. Need I say any more. Why could the week not just start on a Tuesday? Nothing good ever came out of Mondays. The day was long; it was tiring and never-ending. My contact with Alex had been minimal, for the first time since she had left for Cannon Beach. Our regular evening phone call had been postponed; we blamed our conflicting schedules. Work kept me even later than a Monday usually did. When I finally arrived home, Alex had gone to bed early after a stressful day of doctor's appointments and uncertainty. That stretched our communication disruption to over 24 hours. The occasional text message did not compare to hearing the raspy voice I loved so much.

The following day our conversation had been all together brief.

"Hey, you."

"Hey Kace, is everything okay?"

The question suggested she was not expecting my phone call.

"Of course, just checking in. I feel like we haven't had a real conversation in forever."

Alex sighed.

"I know, and I am about to cut it short again. We are just about to take Rose to the drive-in cinema. I told you earlier, didn't I?"

She had failed to mention her evening plans, unlike her.

"Oh, I don't think you did. That sounds like a lot of fun, though. We can talk when you get home?"

"Yeah, it's something she wanted to do. She hasn't been to a drive-in cinema since the '70s, so she is super excited."

Another small but meaningful request ticked off Rose's bucket list. I heard Natalie shouting to check if they needed to stop for gas.

"I bet the picture quality is a lot better than it was in the'70s." I joked.

"Oh, for sure! Nat wants me, Kace, we have a few pit-stops to make before the film starts so I have to go, but I will call you tomorrow, okay? I love you."

The hope of speaking to her at the end of the night diminished.

"Okay, have a fun time. I love you too."

The phone call ended, and I was left wanting more. Uncertain about our current situation, I forced the feelings of doubt away and continued with my evening.

The short-lived chat meant that almost three days had passed without a substantial conversation, something that was unfamiliar. Alex was mediocre when it came to sending text messages, surprisingly the only thing after four months that I could find fault with. She had quickly brought it to my attention within the first week of us knowing one another, old fashioned as it may be, she preferred to speak on the phone; therefore not speaking seemed even more challenging because that was fundamental to our communication.

The longer we went without conversing, the less real our relationship felt. The seed of doubt that had been planted days earlier began to bloom, and the anxiety that swept through my body was nauseating. All hope now riding on my trip to Oregon, I told myself I would make arrangements at work the next day. We needed to see each other to remember just how intense and undeniable our connection was. I loved her, I needed her, I wanted her, more than anything, but did Alex still feel the same way? That was the question at the forefront of my mind.

CHAPTER SEVEN

On reflection, the contemplations that will go through your mind at the first sign of insecurity or doubt are remarkable. I loved Alex; that was clear to me and anyone that knew me. Whilst deliberating with myself over the brief period me and Alex did not speak, I asked myself three provocative questions.

What if our circumstance stayed the same way for another six months or even a year?

Would we make it through that?

What about when she came back with a heavy heart from the loss of her beloved grandma? Would she still be the same person I had fallen so deeply in love with?

The conclusion I came to was one of two halves. One month prior, I would have said yes, without hesitation, we would make it, and if anything, we would become stronger for it, but as the days rolled on and our contact became less frequent, I felt like she was slipping away.

It was the 21st of October. We had been separated from one another the same amount of time we had been together. That was a sad realisation. I could only assume that Alex felt none of the reservations I did. She went about her daily routine; there was no sign of uneasiness in her messages, no sign of bleakness when she spoke. That led me to believe that maybe it was just me. It would not be the first time I had over analysed a situation.

After a gruelling day at work, I lay in bed and found myself reminiscing. Alex had taken it upon herself to compose an e-mail three weeks into her time at Cannon Beach. Her reasoning being, she had not been able to sleep and the only thoughts that occupied her mind were of me. Therefore she wanted to write them down so I could read them too.

At the time, it had filled me with such a sense of satisfaction and overpowering love that was unfamiliar to me.

It went like this;

Kacy,
I lay in bed tonight, and my mind is overrun with thoughts of you. I love you so much, despite our brief time together. You have fast become one of the most important people in my life.
I hope that you realise your importance to me and how incredibly hard it has been to be apart from you. Despite the miles between us, I am always here for you, and I promise I will only ever strive to make you happy.
You bring out the best parts of me; I see that clearly now. Natalie said the same thing to me yesterday. She is already becoming tired of my constant ramblings about how much I miss you, how perfect you are, and the future I plan for us to have. Rose is a little more willing to listen.
The night I met you was undoubtedly the best night of my life. Meeting you gave me a reason to believe in all the beautiful things this world has to offer. I was lost and unhappy before I met you, life had kicked me one too many times, and now everything is different.
I intend on staying in your life for a long time, providing you will have me, of course. If I am lucky, that will be forever. Some will say we are crazy for talking of forever after a mere three

months, but I know this is different.
I will try and sleep now. Maybe I will get the pleasure of a dream filled with you.
I love you.
Alex

Surely someone who wrote those heartfelt words only five weeks prior must have still felt the same way. The reassurance I had been looking for was right there in front of my eyes. Five weeks was a long time. Everything then had been glorious, the strain was minimal, and the love between us had been at its pinnacle. The e-mail did not become what I hoped it would, a sudden awareness that everything I had been worrying about was non-existent. Only a conversation with Alex would be able to put my mind at ease.

I had tried to call Alex on my dinner break earlier that day, but there had been no answer. I wanted to tell her that I missed her, that I loved her, and I just wanted everything to go back to normal. I wanted to believe that it was all in my head and that nothing had changed between us. The speech I had planned disappeared when the phone rang through to her voicemail. It was unusual, but I assumed she was on an important call and she would call me back.

Three hours went by, and I still had no response. I called her again, straight to voicemail. Why was her phone off? Was her battery dead again? I had no other way of contacting her other than her mobile phone. I did not have her sister's number, so the option to contact Natalie if I needed too was not available. Alex's behaviour had changed and it was driving me insane.

I recalled the conversation from the night before.

"We met up with a few women that Rose knew from probably 15-20 years ago today. It was the happiest I have seen her in a long time; I think it tops everything we have done so far since we have been here. There was this one woman called Evelyn, and what a character she was. She had me in stitches with tales of her and my grandma."

"That is amazing, Alex. I am so happy for Rose. It sounds like she's been having a great time. Do you have any plans for tomorrow?"

"I think we might take Rose to see a theatre show. Jennifer's best friend works there, so she can get free tickets to any show we want. How cool is that?"

The theatre show. Is that why her phone was off? That made sense, but the failure to tell me what time it started or that she would be unavailable was strange. Details that she usually would have shared seemed to slip her mind suddenly.

What puzzled me the most was the lack of communication since the night before. I had briefly spoken to her on the phone at 6 pm. That is when she had informed me of her potential theatre plans the next day, but at the same time, her plans that very evening were temperamental and shifty. She and Natalie were going to a local bar for a few drinks, but Natalie had not been feeling too great since lunch, so the evening could have gone either way. There had been no communication to say she had gone or when she had returned home. My message the morning after had gone unanswered, and then two unanswered phone calls. Something did not feel right.

The way in which she frequently mentioned Jennifer's name made me anxious. She had spent a significant amount of time with her in some form or another since they had re-connected.

Was that the reason she was distant?

Had she found someone else to occupy her time?

Was Jennifer making advances toward Alex? The thought of her being around my girlfriend more than I could angered me. I had to pull myself together. I had no evidence nor any reason to question Alex, hence why I kept any theories to myself. I didn't know Jennifer; she more than likely had nothing but good intentions. I could only go off what Alex had told me, and I trusted her judgement.

What I needed primarily was to contact Alex. Once I explained, I was sure she would tell me the scenarios I had played out in my head were fictitious and a complete self-sabotage mission. They had to be.

I tried to continue with the rest of my evening. My dinner was not at all appetising. I shied away from conversation with my family and Whitney when she called. I tried to push everything to the back of my mind as best I could, which proved difficult.

My work was calling from my desk on the opposite side of the room. I had to concentrate on the new block of apartments I was designing. After the success of my first building design, my boss felt it necessary to give me more of a challenge, something he had never done before with an intern, especially not an intern who had only been at the company a mere two months. I had been trusted with designing an upscale, high-class block of apartments, standing eight floors tall with two penthouse suites at the very top and a middle floor that held a bar, restaurant, gym, and a swimming pool.

The description of what the company wanted was extravagant; for one apartment, the price tag was in the region of $500,000. My dad had designed similar buildings throughout the course of his career, which was a bonus for me. I always had him for any support or advice, which made me feel at ease with taking on such a big project.

Work occupied my mind for a brief period. I finished all I could achieve that night at around 8 pm, and I still had no reply from Alex, no missed call, not even a text to say sorry I missed your call. The signal was unreliable at the best of times, so I would generally let her off for the late replies, but this was different; something didn't sit right.

Panic overcame me. In one last ditched attempt to get an answer, I tried her again. This time her phone did not go straight to voicemail. After four rings, an unfamiliar voice answered.

"ALEX!!" I yelled.

"Hello, this isn't Alex."

Replied a voice I did not recognise.

"Oh, sorry, is Alex there please?"

Who was that? Instant confusion.

"No, sorry, this is Jennifer. Alex is not here; she left her phone at my house last night. I can let her know you called when she comes back if you like? She should be here soon."

Jennifer? Why had Alex been at Jennifer's house? My heart sank into my stomach.

"Oh, okay, yeah, just tell her that Kacy tried calling please."

I was frozen in place, the burning in my stomach unbearable.

"Of course, no problem Kacy. You enjoy the rest of your evening."

She sounded like an automated service. Her tone of voice was so readable and false; she wanted me to know she was not sincere.

What on earth was happening? I told myself not to jump to the most obvious conclusion, not until I had the chance to speak to Alex. I was sure she would clear it all up and put it down to one extensive misunderstanding. Wishful thinking perhaps.

I lay awake until after midnight; still, I had no response from Alex. She was supposedly returning to Jennifer's, so she should have picked up her phone and noticed my abundance of messages and phone calls throughout the day. Even if that was not the case, surely, she wanted to speak to me? Surely something in her mind would be calling out for me, considering it was all we had known for close to five months.

I refused to wait up any longer, nor would I put myself through the agonising discomfort that came with the unknown. I told myself I was stronger than that. If Alex did not contact me the next day and explain everything, I would have my answer.

Surely, I deserved the truth. She owed me that.

CHAPTER EIGHT

JOURNAL ENTRY 22/10/2010

I have never felt this way before; no one has ever made my heart ache to this extent. I cannot understand it anymore. Why is Alex being so different with me? Why suddenly is there no contact from her? What have I done wrong?
If Jennifer has something to do with this, if Alex has fallen in love with someone else, just tell me!! Why would she not just tell me? I thought Alex was different.
I did not believe for one second she could hurt me like this. I should have known that everything was too perfect to be true that she was too perfect. I put her on such a high pedestal, so maybe it is my fault. I let my guard down too easily, and now I have to pay the price.
There is nothing else I can do now.
Alex has been so inevitable to me from the moment I met her. She is the love of my life, the reason for my existence, or at least I thought she was.
I guess things change.

My journal entries since meeting Alex had been blissful. In fact, they were more than that; they were entries about love, passion, creativity, and beauty. Everything that I had rediscovered since I met her. Emotions that soon evaporated from the pages before me, fading one by one as I carved out a new path for my journal. The only words I could fathom lacked inspiration, they portrayed unhappiness, and I made no effort to change that.

When I heard nothing from Alex after my phone call with Jennifer, I took it upon myself to assume that whatever we had once shared was a lie. Alex's deceit had been discovered. She did not want me to know she had been at Jennifer's, nor did she expect me to find out. She had been careless, irresponsible. Was she playing us both? Maybe Jennifer was just as much of a victim as I was. Who was to say Alex had told her about me? Alex could have been keeping both her options firmly open. That was not the person I knew. I told myself my Alex would not behave like that, but what other explanation was there? My heart continued to defend her, finding the vulnerable snippet of hope that remained, but my head knew better.

Why should I tolerate what was happening as if it was acceptable? How dare she think she could throw me to the curb as if I meant nothing to her. The rage within me grew as the clock hands ticked, no phone calls, no text messages, no explanations. In one last-ditch attempt to get a reply, I called again; eventually, it went to voicemail. My temper boiling, I sent a text message demanding an answer.

Why are you not talking to me? What have I done wrong? Is this because of Jennifer? Is that all it took to push me to the side as if I meant nothing to you? The least you could do is talk to me. Surely you owe me that. I never took you for the sort of person to just ghost someone, not someone you claimed to be so truly in love with. I am stunned beyond belief.

Shock radiated through my whole body when I received a reply 10 minutes later.

I am sorry.

Disbelief. Devastation. Was that it? A simple I am sorry was all I deserved. A numbness coated my whole body; my worst fears were found to be true. It was even more soul-destroying than I thought possible. Alex considered me so disposable that she did not feel the need to comfort me. She did not feel the need to let me down gently or beg for my forgiveness. That was the cruellest part. A basic courtesy that she found impossible to grant me. I climbed into bed. Broken. Tired. Unable to fight the tears any longer. I had my answer.

The following day the burden from the night before was heavy on my heart. My eyes carried the weight of the world after hours of sobbing. There was only one person that would be able to make sense of the situation, Whitney. In times of crisis, she knew exactly how to rationalise, so when I picked up my phone that morning, the number I dialled was without hesitation.
"Hey girl, are you not at work?"
The surprise to see me calling at 11 am on a weekday was real.
"Hey Whit, no, I took the day off. I needed some time to process things, and they owed me a couple of days."
My boss had been incredibly forthcoming in granting me two days off at such short notice. A thank you for all the demanding work he said. It meant I had a long weekend off work, something I so desperately needed.
"Still no word from Alex then?"
Unfortunately.

"That's why I was calling. I sent a text message last night, and she replied."

Whitney gasped, surprised.

"You are kidding? Well, what did she say? Tell me everything."

I had hoped for more to tell.

"I am sorry."

Whitney paused, waiting for more.

"Sorry for what? Why are you saying sorry?"

My vague approach did not hit home.

"That is all she said. I am sorry."

"Wait. What? Her reply to your message was '*I am sorry*' and that's it?"

The tears formed again.

"Literally just that, no explanation, no answers to any of my questions. It is as if I meant nothing to her. That is what hurts the most."

I began to sob.

"I cannot believe her. I do not understand why anyone would act that way. How dare she. I am so sorry, Kace. Sorry that she did not even have the decency to give you an explanation."

The anger in Whitney's voice resonated. She felt my pain.

"I think I am still in shock. I rechecked social media this morning. Jennifer posted for the first time in four months, and it was a picture of her and her friends. Alex was in the picture too. The caption…"

My voice broke as I tried to finish what I needed to say.

"…it said *'to new beginnings'* and a heart. Is she trying to destroy me? What kind of a woman does that?"

The pain was unbearable.

"She is a sorry excuse of a woman; that is what she is. I suppose we don't know how much Jennifer knows, so Alex is the one to blame here. Unless it turns out Jennifer knew she had a girlfriend and still pursued Alex anyway, well then she is just an all-around bitch."

Whitney's emphasis on the last word spoke volumes. The thought of Alex with another woman, excruciating.

"No, you are right, I hate her, but I don't know if she is the one I should be hating. I know you are going to tell me to stop looking at social media, but it is all so raw right now, I physically can't help myself."

It is precisely what I would have told Whitney if the shoe were on the other foot.

"You know that is exactly what you need to stop doing. We have all been there, Kace. It will consume your life if you let it."

Whitney's following statement was exactly what I would have expected.

"This is what I want you to do. I want you to listen to me very carefully. You are going to go onto social media, search for Alex and Jennifer and block them both. In fact, add her sister to that list as well if she's on there. This is not good for you; you will drive yourself insane. I know it is early days, and I know this is such a shock right now, but you need to take steps to move forward, and I will be here with you every step of the way."

It seemed like a drastic step.

"I don't know if I can do that, Whit. Is it not better to know what she's doing? Maybe, that will help me move on. "

I was kidding myself. Whitney would see straight through me I thought.

"Of course you can! No, and you know for a fact it is not better to know. You are sabotaging your healing if you choose to look for things that will hurt you on a daily basis. I know it seems hard right now, but you will thank me later."

She was correct; I had no time to respond.

"Put me on loudspeaker right now and do it. Trust me, Kace, it needs to be done. Do not make me drive to your house and do it myself because you know I will."

Tough love was something that came naturally to Whitney. I did as she asked, placed her on loudspeaker, clicked onto social media and searched for Jennifer's name. That would be the easiest one to start with.

"Are you doing it?"

"Yes."

I blocked Jennifer. Natalie did not have one, so that was easy. That left me with one last search in order to complete the request. Alex Dawson, I pondered. How had it come to this? How did I find myself removing traces of you from my life bit by bit? Whitney remained silent as I gathered the courage to do what had to be done.

"It's done." I wept.

"Good. I am proud of you. Now take a breath, compose yourself. Wipe those tears away and remember you are strong Kace, you can get through this."

I pulled a tissue from my bedside table; there was no shortage after the night before. Whitney continued.

"Are you ready for task number two?"

I was not, but I knew she would leave me no choice.

"You have been waiting a long time to upgrade your phone, yes?"

"Yes, I have been meaning to get around to it. Why?"

Unsure of the relevance. It was not the time to talk about new technology.

"Good, then I will meet you at the mall today, and we will upgrade it together. You can get yourself a new number, and at the same time, you can remove Alex from your contact list."

"Seriously?"

The tone in her voice made it clear just how serious she was.

"Do you want to have the temptation for you to get drunk one night and humiliate yourself? You know that will happen, you remember when Chad broke up with me? We all know how badly that went, and if I could go back now and tell myself to do what I am asking you to do, I would. Besides, it also means she cannot contact you and hurt you even more."

The thought made me feel physically sick. The Chad story resonated with me at that moment. I had witnessed Whitney's heartbreak. I had also seen her make a complete fool out of herself on more than one occasion, she learnt from that, and her growth was now the source of my advice.

"I understand, believe me, but do you think it might be a little too soon?"

I was stalling, my mind still fighting between the right thing to do and the easiest thing to do. Whitney's response was as blunt as ever.

"Absolutely not. This girl has done you wrong, and believe me, one day soon she will realise how big of a mistake she has made and when she does, do you know what you will be doing?"

No, but I knew she would tell me before I even had the chance to respond.

"You will be living your life to the best of your ability, completely Alex free, and that is the best revenge you can ever have."

That was far from what I wanted to be doing. Revenge and Alex should not have been in the same sentence, but that is when I found myself asking, Did I really have a choice?

"I know you are right; it just does not make this any easier."
I exhaled.

"I know that, Kace, but that is what I am here for, to help you through times like this. In all seriousness, it might seem extreme to delete her number and change yours, but if she does not have the decency to treat you with the respect you deserve, then has she left you any other choice? You need to show her that Kacy Sullivan pines for nobody, and she certainly does not let a girl ruin her life."

Fighting words from Whitney. She was my right hook when I could barely get off the canvas. My energy was at an all-time low.

"Thank you for always being there for me. I love you."

"Ditto boo, now meet me at the mall in an hour."

Two hours later, I had a new phone and a new phone number. Alex was no longer in my contacts. It was symbolic, in a way, an enormous decision to make.

"Do you think I have been too hasty?"

I looked to Savannah, who had joined us at the mall for moral support and to play the devil's advocate role.

"I think it's brave, and it takes a lot of guts to do what you have done. I honestly don't think I would have the strength to do that. You are doing the best you can to move forward, and most people would envy you for being able to do that with such conviction."

It was by far the hardest thing I had ever had to do in 21 years of my life. To remove the person I truly loved from my world, piece by piece, was excruciating. I tried to keep my composure; I made out as though I was strong enough to do it, but deep down inside, I was broken. I knew the moment I arrived home; I would cry to myself uncontrollably.

"Thanks Savannah, you always know what to say."

My best friends, what a blessing.

"I still cannot believe it; it doesn't add up, does it. After everything you told us about the two of you and how great things were going. I just can't make sense of it."

That made two of us. All my friends agreed; the moves Alex had made were cowardly and unjustified. They wanted answers as much as I did.

"I know."

The strength to talk about it was diminishing.

"Whitney will probably hate me for this, but maybe you should not give up so easily. If it were me, I would probably make a massive fool of myself and fly out to Oregon to get some answers. I am not saying I want you to make a fool of yourself, obviously, but is doing it this way going to get you the closure you need?"

Savannah had a point. She had always been more rational than Whitney; having both of their opinions and advice was helpful but also extremely confusing. Whitney rolled her eyes, so blatantly obvious. Surprisingly, she kept quiet.

"I don't think I could put myself through that. My pride is telling me I can't be that desperate girl that fly's across the country to plead for someone to take them back."

Whitney smiled before she added her two pence worth.

"That's my girl. You are a strong, courageous, confident, and beautiful woman. You do not need Alex Dawson, and you certainly do not need to beg anyone for anything."

I smiled for the first time that day, even if it was somewhat forced. I struggled to believe I was any of the things Whitney described, but I vowed to make sure that nobody would suspect any different.

"You are right, I could not think of a better four words to describe Kacy, but the closure?" added Savannah.

We looked toward each other, taking a moment to contemplate, rarely was there silence between us. Closure is something that comes with time, but something that may never come if there is no resolution to the ending of a relationship. That was the worry. Would I always be wondering what happened?

"Closure is different for everyone, Kace. I assume one day she will return to Raleigh. Maybe then that is when you fully get your closure, but until then, you do everything in your power to cut emotional ties with her starting with what we have done today."

Whitney was right. I was scared about my ability to move on, knowing I did not have all the answers, but I had no choice. The possibility of Alex returning to Raleigh had been absent from my train of thought. If she were ever to come back, I had to make sure she would never know of the way my heart had broken into a million pieces. I would not allow her the satisfaction of knowing I stayed up crying all night, struggling to sleep because my mind would not allow thoughts of her to subside. If she returned, I would be the strong, confident woman my friends described me to be, with little to no trace of the pain she had caused. That is what I hoped anyway.

"The thought of her returning to Raleigh has knocked me sick. I didn't think about that, but of course she will eventually, she owns a bar here and her apartment."

What if she returned with Jennifer? I asked myself. That was something I would not be mentally prepared for. Would I go to her bar one day for a drink and see her with Jennifer, all cosy as if I never existed. The picture in my head proved stubborn.

"Maybe she will, but that is something we can deal with when the time comes. You do not live close to her. It is not like you have to see her, and we can avoid her bar like the plague. I will not be lining her pockets after this mess; I don't care how nice the food is." Whitney scorned.

How did I find myself in a position where I would have to avoid the person I thought I would spend the rest of my life with?

"This is so hard. Oh god, I still have her house key and a

bunch of my things there. I didn't even think about that."

How was I supposed to contact her now to arrange the collection of my belongings?

"Then we will go together and get them. She's not here, so it doesn't matter. We will nip in quickly, gather your stuff and leave her key once we are done." Chimed Whitney.

The thought of entering Alex's apartment made my palms sweat. I turned back to Whitney.

"Can we leave that for another day though? I do not have the energy to do that today."

Truth be told, I knew it would break me. I was not ready for that step, even though it was inevitable. Whitney smiled tenderly and put her arm around my shoulder, Savannah put her arm around my waist from the opposite side, and we strolled towards the mall's exit linked together as one. My ultimate support bubble, by my side, ready to take on the world.

CHAPTER NINE

It was the 1st of November. The air was crisp and dark, temperatures had begun to drop, and the North Carolina winter was setting in. Over a week had passed since I last had contact with Alex. The difficult part was not knowing. Had she tried to contact me? Or had she just forgotten my existence altogether?

A simple explanation would have gone a long way. I thought about how that would play out daily. What would she have said? What excuses would she have used? Would she have seemed sincere and regretful? Or not at all. The thoughts were always there, but I refused to let them ruin me.

My mom had been my rock. She had a sixth sense when it came to my emotions. My sadness and anxiety was apparent to her before it was me, and she would always find a way to cheer me up. We spent every evening since the break-up talking, eating junk food, and crying at romantic comedies. Any of my friends would have been great company for such a pity party, and Whitney even joined on two occasions, but there was nothing quite like having your mom by your side to comfort you in the hardest of times. She was my first ever best friend, and that would never change.

My bedroom became my safe haven, my place of healing,

but after a week of the same four walls, my mom felt it was time to re-energise, relax and unwind. The only way to truly do that was with a spa day.

A Full Monty treatment included skincare, nail-care, a massage, a manicure, and a pedicure. When you add in lunch and champagne in between treatments, it was a glorious day out. Being pampered all day long had to be the ultimate way to loosen up and let go of any tension. I did not need to be asked twice. Sign me up, I expressed. It did not take away the aching in my chest, but it was a much-needed distraction, and allowing time for yourself never did hurt anyone.

Michelle did not pry for details, I had already told her what I felt was necessary, and that was all she required. The instant dislike she took towards Alex had been hard at first; instinctively I had to stop myself from defending her. Unconsciously I still wanted to protect her; love can do peculiar things to you.

"Thank you for today, mom."

It was the third time I had thanked her since we arrived.

"Any time, sweetheart. You know we do not need an excuse to use your father's credit card though."

She laughed. The spa day was courtesy of my father, who's opinion on the situation had been minimal. That was not a surprise, my dad liked to listen, but he left the advice to my mom. They worked well in that sense.

"Mom, can I ask you something?"

She nodded, touching the tip of the champagne flute to her lips for the last time; a refill was in order.

"Before you met dad, did you ever get your heart broken?"

She smiled softly.

"Oh, of course, I don't think you will meet anyone that has not experienced heartbreak in one form or another, sweetheart."

I sat patiently, hoping she would share her story.

"There was a boy named Charlie. He was your typical quarterback of the football team. Very popular, but not unkind. He had a smart head on his shoulders, and that is what attracted me to him. He was very handsome, had all these aspirations to see the world. We dated for two years. Then it was time to go off to college. We tried to see each other most weekends and on the holiday's, but we only lasted until the end of freshman year."

"What happened? Why did you break up?"

I probed.

"One of my close friends went to the same college, and they told me they had seen him with another girl. He started being distant, and eventually, he told me the truth that he had met someone else."

"Wow, that must have been rough. How did you cope?"

I had so many questions about my mom's experience, asking in the hope I would find some answers, a moment of clarity, maybe a glimmer of hope that might fuel the optimism I longed for.

"Initially, I thought my world was going to end as any normal 19-year-old would. It wasn't easy. He was my high school sweetheart. Everyone thought we would get married and have children. We were prom King and Queen; the couple voted most likely to stay together forever. Looking back now, we had a lot of pressure put on us at such a young age. I saw him two years later, and it was even hard then, but you move forward, you find distractions, and eventually it gets easier."

She leaned over and pulled the champagne from the saturated ice bucket.

"Re-fill?"

"Yes, please."

Deep conversations required alcohol.

"So that must have been tough, huh? If you saw him two years later and you still felt some type of emotion. I suppose I don't have much hope in getting over Alex anytime soon?"

That was my fear.

"I won't lie to you, it wasn't easy, but shortly after that encounter, I met your father, and everything fell into place. Charlie became irrelevant after that because I knew I had met my soulmate. I guess what I am trying to say is, emotions are temporary, the pain you feel now will not go away instantly, but it will go away eventually. One day someone will come along and make you realise that the person who broke your heart did not deserve it in the first place."

How did she always make such perfect sense, I thought.

"So basically, the Charlie's of the world are learning curves, but the George's, they are end game?"

Michelle laughed. A lesson of sorts had been learnt even if I did put my own spin on it.

"Thank you, mom, for always being there for me."

She squeezed my hand.

"Always, seven days a week, 24 hours a day, that is what I am here for."

We raised our glasses, cheers to that. The masseuse called us back for our second treatment. All my worries would drift away temporarily as I allowed myself to cherish the experience and the short-lived solace I acquired.

The following day I met Whitney at her house. She had been pleading with me to see her revamped bedroom for two whole days. A recent renovation meant Whitney had been given free rein to do as she pleased, according to her parents. My knock on the door, answered instantly.

"Look at you all zen and what not. You look like a new woman."

I rolled my eyes playfully before pulling her in for a hug. Her hair was different, more luxurious than normal; she had been to the salon.

"You are so full of shit, but thanks! Have you been to the salon without me? Your hair looks insane."

I ran my fingers through the ends of her luscious red curls.

"I may have taken a trip this morning. I had some time on my hands, so what is a girl to do? You know I love a good blow-dry."

The blow-dry usually constituted a night out or a date.

"Well, you look incredible anyway."

"Thanks, boo! So, how was your spa day with the famous mama M?"

Whitney ushered me towards the stairs, and I followed the familiar route up to her bedroom.

"Beautiful, tranquil, everything it should have been. I slept better last night than I have done in weeks, so that was a bonus."

She stalled as we reached her bedroom door, ready for the big reveal.

"Sounds amazing. Are you ready?"

"As ready as I will ever be."

Whitney had two large wooden doors that opened into her bedroom. It was not your typical bedroom or your regular size, for that matter. Whitney had been begging her parents to knock through into one of the adjoining guest rooms for years so she could have a bigger room and more space for her ever-growing closet. Granted, she could have just stopped buying clothes, but her parents spending thousands on a renovation was, of course, more appealing to Whitney.

Her bedroom had doubled in size. A giant queen-sized bed became the focal point, next to the balcony window on the far wall. There was office space in one corner of the room with a large white desk that housed her computer. At the other side, another set of wooden doors opened into a walk-in wardrobe big enough for her clothes and mine combined. Her face lit up with pride at that point.

There was a giant TV on the wall with a seating area that would easily entertain six people. It was all perfectly decorated with a soft pink and pastel grey theme. It had Whitney written all over it, and I was pleasantly surprised by what a great job she had done.

"So, what do you think?"

"Honestly, I think it looks incredible. It is everything you used to talk about and more. That closet is spectacular, like seriously look at the size of that thing."

I wandered inside, completely in awe. It was to die for.

"Well, I figured, a girl can never have too many clothes, so better to have too much space than not enough."

We circled the room several times. I asked questions and showed interest in the artwork chosen and the reasons behind certain aspects of the room. In all honesty, I was stalling. I knew where our conversation would lead, the same place it had done every day for two weeks. The day after I deleted Alex from my life, Whitney turned up at my house with an extra-large tub of ice cream and a bag full of chocolate. Whitney was invasive on occasion, but she was by far the best friend anyone could ever hope for.

"So, have you heard from Alex at all?"

She was sympathetic in her approach. It was courtesy to ask, but surely, she must have known I would tell her instantly if I did.

"No. The only way she could contact me now would be via email, and she hasn't done that, so I guess I was right all along."

Whitney sat down on her new grey leather sofa and

signalled for me to get comfortable beside her.

"Email? Do you think she would email?"

"I think if she really wanted to get in contact with me, she would. I have told you she sent me that one email in the past, and I used to send bits of my work over to her so it would not be unusual."

"I should have made you block her email too."

I laughed. I predicted that response.

"I am not checking it every five minutes, so don't panic. What is done is done. I guess you never really know someone as well as you think you do."

Whitney grabbed my arm as if she had just discovered something otherworldly.

"Do you know what amazing friends like me do? We take our best friends out on the town to help them recover from broken hearts. We need to find you a distraction. It would be a crime for a hot piece of ass like yourself just to stay indoors and pine."

I regularly wondered how Whitney stayed so upbeat all the time. However she did it, I was thankful for her. She made me feel so much better about everything, and for that, I would be eternally grateful.

"I am just not sure I want a distraction. The thought of entertaining anyone romantically does not interest me in the slightest, but of course, as always, I appreciate your efforts to try and cheer me up."

A night out with Whitney was always eventful, the ones I remembered anyway.

"I get that, but you just never know, do you? Let me be your distraction then, platonically, of course. As hot as you are, I am just not into you like that."

I hurled a cushion at Whitney; amused with herself, she beamed from ear to ear.

"So, is that a yes?"

Did I have a choice? I thought.

"It is a strong possibility. What do you have in mind?"

It took her all of 10 seconds to think of a plan.

"I am thinking this Friday we go to Icon, pre-drinks at your place, of course. I will do all the inviting, and I will even supply the drinks; the cellar here is fully stocked, so that will not be an issue. We will go to the mall this afternoon to pick up a new outfit. Nothing too over the top, though, if I remember right, Icon is very casual on a Friday night, isn't it? We still need you to look absolutely fierce, though, which comes naturally to you."

Whitney paused for breath. She was awaiting my response to her well thought out plan.

"Yes, more casual definitely. Icon sounds good, it has been a while since we went, and I think I would prefer to avoid Club Fifteen."

Otherwise known as the place I met Alex Dawson.

"I already have some new clothes, though. I overindulged last month, remember?"

Whitney was routing through her wardrobe for something unknown to me.

"Oh yeah, you got some really cute stuff…where is that new bag I bought…"

Whitney's wardrobe despite being new, was far from organised.

"So, do you want to swing by my place one night this week, and you can help me pick something out?"

Giving Whitney the pleasure of choosing my outfit would be like music to her ears.

"Sounds perfect Kace. Now, come over here and help me find this damn bag."

I made a mental note to help Whitney re-organise her closet

on my next day off.

The more I thought about a night out with my friends, the more I began to look forward to it. I would try to avoid Club Fifteen; that was my only reservation. The place I met Alex filled me with memories of a happier time, mix that with alcohol, and it would not be good for anyone. I wanted to enjoy myself, not weep in a corner.

Pre-drinks were always at my house. I had a second lounge with a bar that rarely got used; another impulse buy on my mother's part. What made it even more hilarious at the time was the fact that neither of my parents drank a great deal. It fast became the place for me to entertain my friends, which I was thankful for.

Friday soon came around. Working 12-hour days often left me wondering where my week had gone. I aspired to work hard in my twenty's and thirty's so I could retire early and enjoy the rest of my life. That was the dream, and that is what I pictured as the overtime hours mounted. Work at that time had also become a refreshing distraction. I would only find myself thinking about Alex every so often. Progress.

Whitney called at my house the night before and helped me pick out a questionable outfit. We decided on some mid-wash skinny jeans, an extremely tight black corset style top, and my cropped leather jacket to finish off the outfit. Accompany that with a pair of black heels and my hair as sleek and as curly as it would allow. Smart casual was a tough category to crack.

When I finished work, a text from Whitney promptly appeared with the details of the evening. The estimated arrival time at my house was 8 pm, the taxi was pre-booked for 10 pm, which left plenty of time for people to arrive and drink. The details included a list of everyone attending, referencing my request of no more than ten people. My parents were cool, but even they had to draw the line somewhere.

The girls coming over to my house beforehand were Savannah, Sophia, Chloe, Jessica, and Lara. The last one I had to double-check with Whitney, it was, in fact, my ex-girlfriend Lara. She and Jessica had formed a close friendship of late, not completely strange to me at the time, considering we all used to hang out together in college. Lara had been present when Whitney asked Jessica, so she extended the invitation. I wondered if that were the whole truth; with Whitney, there would often be an unknown motive. Either way, Lara's presence was a welcome one. When I checked my phone after going through Whitney's itinerary, I had a text from Lara.

Hey Stranger.
I am looking forward to a good night out tonight, I hope it is okay to come over to yours with everyone else. I feel like I have not seen you in forever.
Let me know if you need me to bring anything over. However, I am positive that Whitney has the drinks covered.
See you later.
Lara

Lara was sweet; I had to give her that. We hadn't crossed paths since my 21st birthday, so I was excited to see her again. Lara was attractive, funny, kind, friendly, and in my head, potentially the perfect distraction. Why had it never actually worked out with her? I asked myself. Strange. When so much time passes, you forget the reasoning.

Chloe was the first to arrive; she was never late or even on time for that matter. Shortly after 8 pm, everyone had arrived. There was an electrifying atmosphere in the room and anticipation that the evening's events would be enjoyable.

With the bar fully stocked and ice buckets at the ready, the drinks were flowing. Whitney had brought an array of beverages, including champagne, white and red wine, gin, vodka, and several mixers. Her family would use any excuse to throw a party, so their basement was always fully stocked with alcohol. Whitney poured me a drink; the level of alcohol to mixer was unthinkable. My sensible side quickly left the party after that, and I knew I would regret it in the morning.

Lara approached me after five minutes. I had to hand it to her; she looked great. Her long blonde hair was tied up in a high ponytail, leaving her facial features on full view. The structure of her cheekbones and jawline were enviable. The skinny jeans and t-shirt combination was a familiar one, all too familiar. I felt nostalgic, the familiar pang in my stomach when I thought about Alex or even worse when something reminded me of her was present.

"Hey, Kacy. I love the set-up."

"Hey, Lara, thank you. Do you need a drink?"

Lara lifted her full glass.

"Whitney already took care of that. Does she always have this much alcohol in her drinks, though? Jeez, it's strong."

She scrunched her face in disgust as she reluctantly took another sip.

"Here, let me add some more soda in that for you. She is a nightmare for it. I think I am actually just drinking straight spirit right now."

I took the glass from her hand and promptly topped it up.

"That should be less harsh now. How are you anyway? What are you up to these days?"

She took another sip of her drink, her face indicating it was bearable.

"That is much better, thank you. Not a great deal, working most of the time to be honest, totally living the dream."

Her sarcasm made me chuckle.

"Where do you work now?"

"I am working at Ralph Lauren, they offered me the manager's job last year, and well, I get a discount off the clothing, so I could hardly say no, could I."

She gestured towards the outfit she was wearing, which was 90% Ralph Lauren products.

"Oh well, I know where to come now then don't I, the next time I need some new clothes."

I winked automatically, surprising myself with the first flirtatious thing I had done in weeks. I was half-joking about the discount; a girls got to take what she can get.

"I can hook you up, don't you worry about that. How are you anyway?"

The question was, how much did Lara know? I assumed Jessica would have told her. My heart started racing at the thought of discussing it. I wanted to have fun; therefore, I would avoid the topic.

"I am good, thank you. Same old really. I rarely do anything other than work these days. At 21, who knew our lives would be so boring."

I nudged her teasingly.

"Depressing, isn't it? Well, I will make you a deal. How about tonight we pretend we are not two of the most boring people on the planet and we try and enjoy ourselves. Nothing is off the table."

She raised her right eyebrow suggestively, awaiting my acceptance of her challenge. I was not sure what '*nothing is off the table*' referred too, but I had nothing to lose.

"Okay, I like that. I am game if you are."

We raised our glasses to the unknown; we all but guaranteed it would be fun.

"I am happy I came tonight." Confessed Lara.

Lara was not the type to beat around the bush; if she wanted something, she would go straight for it. I was altogether aware of that trait because, at one time, I was the something she had wanted. Our conversation was innocent, at least to the observing eye. The look she possessed and the way she ran her fingers down my arm as I clinked my glass to hers said otherwise.

"Me too. It's refreshing."

I supplied Lara with a second drink and disposed of the empty glass in her hand; it consisted of bourbon and cola. I remembered from when we used to date that it was her favourite. She glanced towards the drink, curiosity in her smile.

"What? You think I don't remember your favourite drink?"

I smiled amorously, hoping desperately that it was still the same, so I did not make a fool of myself.

"I am impressed, Kace."

Luckily for me, it was. I felt a shiver run down my spine at the intimate way she said my name. I continued to talk to Lara until the taxi arrived. I received more than one inquiring look from my friends. Whitney pulled me hastily to one side as we left.

"Looks like inviting Lara was my best idea yet."

She winked.

"Oh, I see. What are you up to Whitney Sawyer?"

She found my bewilderment amusing.

"Nothing at all, but if a very fine young woman who happens to be single gets along splendidly with another fine young woman who also happens to be single. What is the harm in that? I say just see where the night takes you."

"Hmmm, I bet you do."

Whitney was about to do everything in her power to make the night more about Lara and me than anything else. After very quickly realising her plan, I would be lying if I said I expected anything less.

The night turned out to be a lot of fun. Old faces filled the bar and some new ones too. My evening was occupied talking to Lara; aside from that, I did nothing but dance the night away. Free as a bird. Alcohol fuelled with my best friends by my side. Like all enjoyable nights out, it was over in the blink of an eye. I was grateful for Whitney, convincing me to go out and selflessly arranging the whole evening. I made a mental note that Icon was indeed the place to be on a Friday night. Even in the midst of heartbreak.

The taxi back to my house arrived at 3 am with Whitney, Jessica, and Lara in tow. We had overindulged on the alcohol front; my body was aware, but so was my purse. When entering the cab, it was evident none of us had sufficient funds for four different drop-offs. That would have been extortionate.

"Okay, so plan B, everyone sleeps at my house?"

It had seemed like an ingenious idea at the time; not once did I think to consult my parents. They would be okay with it; I told myself, as long as nobody threw up on the carpets.

"Are you sure?"

Jessica slurred. That had been my biggest worry, Jessica's inability to keep the alcohol down. There was always that one friend.

"Sure, Whitney will jump in with me; you two can take the guest room."

So, I gladly offered the spare bedroom at my house. Whitney would have more than likely slept at my house anyway; she often did. So it was only two extra people. That is how I justified it.

"Just please try not to make any noise. My dad will have Golf in the morning, and if he scores a bad goal or whatever, then I will be to blame."

I did not understand golf, a strange sport. It always seemed rather dull when my dad spoke about it. Was it a goal? Or a touchdown? Or the thing named after a bird? Like I said, strange.

"I swear I will be on my best behaviour."

Swear sounded like slur, and best sounded like breast. Slightly concerning. I handed her the bottle of water I had acquired from the bar before we left and hoped for the best. Whitney was already nodding off in the backseat, and Lara propping Jessica up with one shoulder, could not help but laugh at the scene before us.

The amount of alcohol consumed that evening was not for the faint-hearted. Jessica immediately collapsed into the spare bed on arrival. Lara, who had thankfully sobered up to a degree, guided her, leaving a bucket at the side of the bed, just in case. My parents would have been proud.

Whitney raised her eyebrow suggestively.

"Don't do anything I wouldn't do."

On collecting a glass of water, she skulked off to get comfortable in my bed.

"But, if you do, make sure you tell me all about it in the morning." She whispered.

Then remained only two; the most responsible and sober two of the bunch left stood in the kitchen to playback the night's events. Had Whitney's plan played out perfectly?

Lara stretched her arms high above her head; a deep yawn followed. Clear signs that she was tired, but there was no immediate attempt to retreat to bed for the night.

"Did you have a nice night?"

I enquired. Two glasses of water at the ready, I handed one to Lara.

"I did. It's been a while since I enjoyed myself that much.

It was nice to see some old faces too."

"It was really nice. Did you get a chance to talk to Olivia? How insane did she look? I haven't seen her in probably three years. I can't believe how much weight she's lost."

Lara gulped, half of the glass gone in one.

"I did probably for about ten minutes towards the end of the night. Did you know she's a fitness model now? She looks unreal."

Olivia Sharpe had been overweight for as long as I could remember. She was often teased for her figure in high school and her inability to partake in gym class. She had always been a sweet girl, and I remembered getting into a scuffle or two with the girls who mistreated her. We sadly lost touch after high school.

"Good for her. She has completely transformed her life, and it's so nice to see."

I joined Lara, who was seated happily at the breakfast bar.

"Thank you for allowing me to stay here tonight." She smiled. "This house brings back some fond memories."

Lara had spent a significant amount of time at my house when we dated. They were carefree times that I found myself longing for.

"We had some good times, didn't we?"

She nodded in agreement.

"We certainly did."

I looked into her eyes; they sparkled under the fluorescent lights. She was beautiful.

"What happened with you and Elena anyway? If you don't mind me asking."

Elena was the girl Lara had dated after me. They were together for two years.

"Nothing major really; it just ran its course. We grew apart, wanted different things, had different interests. Kind of like you and me, I suppose. It seems I am the Queen of mediocre relationships."

I gasped, instantly offended. I playfully hit her leg as I subconsciously shifted to the edge of my seat. The space between us closing slightly.

"Excuse me."

Lara laughed, the uncontrollable outburst louder than anticipated. I rapidly positioned my hand over her mouth.

"Ssshhh...if you wake my parents, I will kill you."

She used her finger to cross her heart.

"Sorry about that. You know what I mean anyway. We weren't mediocre; that was the wrong choice of word."

My hand had slipped from her mouth and lay comfortably on her thigh. The intimacy of the gesture noticeable.

"Can I let you in on a secret?"

I was intrigued. Secrets when intoxicated meant the truth.

"Always."

She didn't hesitate or break eye contact.

"At one point, I thought you were the one that got away. I thought about you a lot throughout my relationship with Elena, but I was too afraid to tell you the truth."

My internal surprise hidden by the calm alcoholic shield clouding my judgement.

"And now?"

She looked puzzled.

"Now what?"

Did I need to spell it out?

"Do you still think I am the one that got away?"

The answer did not matter. I wanted the attention; I craved her attention, a sensation I was unaccustomed to of late.

"That would be telling. Who knows though eh, people have a way of finding their way back to each other."

She was sincere. My body moved an inch closer to hers.

Palms sweaty. The sensation in my body building. Lara leaned in, softly whispering.

"Alex was a fool for letting you go."

The elephant in the room. The person I had managed to avoid thinking about for the duration of the night. Lara had been curious, trying to broach the subject on two occasions. My immediate response to swiftly move on. On the second attempt, I had told her briefly that long-distance had not worked out, and I did not speak any further on the topic. That way there would be no awkwardness and no pity.

She was a fool. Lara was right. Now I had an opportunity to help myself move forward. The familiar question that Savannah had posed; how could I possibly gain any closure from the situation?

The first step was sat in front of me, leaning towards me, parting her lips and smelling heavenly. Lara Manning, in all her glory, was the ultimate closure. Contrary to popular belief, maybe I did not need acknowledgement and explanations, but instead excitement and seduction, the promise that life simply moves on. There was only one way to find out.

CHAPTER TEN

The night did not end at 4 am when I finally declared I was going to bed. It ended at 6 am with me in the second guest room accompanied by Lara. Our bodies may well have been filled with an incredible amount of alcohol, but that did not contribute in the slightest for me; my vision was unclouded. Lara was familiar to me, our sexual connection still pure, that had never been the problem. In fact, that was the one thing we had been reluctant to relinquish.

Regret did not overcome me, much to my astonishment. I was only human, after all. It had been over three months since my last sexual encounter. An encounter I preferred to give little to no thought. That morning was categorized in my mind as a simple act of passion that was too overwhelming for two human beings to deny.

I lay there in her arms afterwards, enjoying the memorable comfort of her body.

"Are you okay? I wasn't expecting that to happen."

Why did people ask if you were okay after sex? I never quite understood that. The weakening in my knees gave me my answer.

"Are you complaining?" I teased.

"Definitely not."

Her smirk indicated she had enjoyed the night just as much as I had.

"Well, I am great, thank you. That was an unexpected but welcome end to the night."

Lara rolled onto her side, propped up by her elbow and ran her fingers down my exposed torso, stopping slowly at the base of my stomach.

"I am wondering why we ever stopped doing that in the first place."

And that was all the encouragement I needed to commence round two.

After my second, even more, intense orgasm. My legs had no life left in them, my body was dripping with sweat, and my breathing began to return to a normal rhythm. I lay there still and quiet, contemplating. The exhaustion beginning to take its toll; what arose shortly after was guilt. Guilt that was not meant for me, guilt I should not sense, but guilt none the less. Overwhelming, earth-shattering, guilt.

A noticeable tear rolled down my cheek, landing on Lara's chest beneath me. Her delicate fingers lifted my head to face hers.

"Kacy, what's wrong?"

"I am just overwhelmed, I guess."

Lara caught the next tear with the tip of her finger.

"Do you want me to leave?"

I felt foolish.

"No, not at all. A part of me just feels guilty, which sounds stupid because I didn't do anything wrong. She was the one who did something wrong."

I realised I had said too much.

"What do you mean? What did she do?"

The night would not end that way. I would not allow our

conversation to become about Alex, especially not with Lara. I cursed Alex in my head for always being at the forefront of my mind.

"Can we talk about that another time? It's not how I want to end the night."

Lara nodded, silently understanding my request.

"This is the most comfortable I have felt in a long time, so thank you for being here with me."

Lara wiped the last remaining tear from my cheekbone and smiled. Inside I felt idiotic, but not because of Lara. She caused no embarrassment, she made me feel like I could feel whatever I needed to feel, and there would be no judgment.

"It's my pleasure. I won't pry for details, but just know you can talk to me if you wish, okay?"

"I know, but shall we get some sleep first?"

The clock on the wall was irrelevant at that point. All I had to do was gaze through the window to my right to see the sun about to rise.

"Yes, please."

I gave her a peck on the cheek and retreated into her arms. The warmth of my dreams finally swept me away.

The following days passed by at a snail's pace. The thought of Alex still firmly occupied my mind. Would there always be that agonizing heartache when I thought of her? My friends assured me that with time I would forget, but I was not altogether convinced.

One month passed, one whole month since we last spoke. Since I received the text message that would end our communication for good. Daily reminders proceeded to show just how meaningful and influential our relationship had been to me anyway. The constant distractions were always welcome as I searched for ways to occupy my mind. Despite it all, deep down, I still wished to see her again. I soon became aware that closure would be difficult to achieve.

Lara's presence became a significant part of my healing. She knew the fragile state I was in; she knew that I was not looking for a relationship or anything remotely complicated. I wanted simplicity, no drama, no arguments, just an easy mutual agreement between two people who above all else enjoyed each other's company. Despite the constant disapproval of the idea from my friends, it had been precisely what Lara had wanted too. Lucky me.

After the initial rendezvous at my house, we continued to see each other, at most two or three times a week. We spent the night together on several occasions, but other times it was nice just to relax and have fun in Lara's company, which was effortless. We made a pact to not make our relationship into something it was not.

My friends made it abundantly clear that it would never work. I was sceptical myself at first, but surprisingly enough for Lara and me, it did. The one person who agreed with me was Whitney, who, in a roundabout way, told me I had needs and I had to do what made me happy at the time. Life was too short to get bogged down worrying about things that may or may not happen. I trusted her judgement most of the time.

It was fast approaching the end of November. My mom was already considering putting up the Christmas decorations, much to my father's dismay. Once I was ready for work, I made my way downstairs. After several months my morning work routine was, by some miracle, under one hour. Believe me, that was a complete and utter marvel. My hair alone on a good day could take 45 minutes to get it just how I liked it. I learnt quickly that it wasn't sustainable so tying it up became much easier and a lot less time-consuming.

The morning rush was probably the most consistent thing in

my life at the time. Despite the fear of being late, I would always find time to spend ten minutes around the breakfast bar with my mom. The morning in question she baked me a chocolate-filled croissant, which, come to think of it, should have sent alarm bells ringing immediately. Who has time to make a pastry from scratch at that time in the morning? The croissant was fresh out of the oven; what a treat. I was nearly 22 years old, but my mom still made me breakfast every morning, did all my washing, ironed my clothes, and made me lunch to take to work. These were just a few perks of living at home. She liked to be needed, and I certainly needed her, so it worked out perfectly for the both of us in my eyes.

Michelle Sullivan appeared different that morning; her usual smiley exterior was less animated. She had even refrained from dressing like she was about to attend a red carpet premiere. That was incredibly unusual.

"Are you okay, Mom? You seem weird."

There was no time to beat around the bush. I had to be leaving for work in precisely 8 minutes.

"I'm fine, Darling. Just feeling a bit tired this morning, that's all."

My instincts alert; she was lying.

"Are you sure that's all? Because you are never tired, beauty sleep is the most important thing, remember?"

Something my mom had drilled into me since I was young, sleep was the difference between having a good or a bad day and looking your best or worst. A powerful thing in her eyes. I gave her a moment to consider telling me whatever was on her mind whilst I devoured the last of my croissant.

"Okay, there is something, but I know you have to go to work, so I wanted to tell you later."

I was immediately concerned. Alert.

"Well, you can't say that and not tell me. You're not ill, are you? Is it Dad? Is Jason okay?"

My mind instantly jumped to the worst possible outcome in my hysteria.

"No, we are all fine, I promise."

She looked at her hands, nervously tugging at the tips of her fingernails.

"It concerns you actually…and…Alex."

Alex? My facial expression turned to one of misunderstanding; surely she didn't mean my Alex. My breathing began to race as she continued.

"Just please try not to get upset with me. I was doing what I thought would be best for you."

She looked towards the floor, regretful. What had she done?

"Mom, seriously, just tell me what is going on."

The palpitations set off. She reached for her handbag on the table and gently pulled out some envelopes, carefully placing each one before me on the countertop. The pacing back and forth began.

"What are these?"

The writing was Alex's; I would have recognised it anywhere.

"Alex sent them."

My hands moved towards the letter's, they were shaking uncontrollably. I looked towards my mom for an explanation.

"I should not have kept them from you, but lately, you have been so much happier. You have been getting on great with Lara, and I didn't want you to get upset again. I know it was not my place, and I feel incredibly guilty about that, which is why I am giving them to you now."

How long had she kept them from me?

"Jesus, I don't understand. How long have you kept these from me?"

Did this mean that all along, Alex had attempted to contact

me? I had to know what was in the letters. Michelle explained.

"The first one came about a week after it all happened. It was a genuine mistake by your father; it got mixed up in some of his post. You know what he's like, it gets put in his office and left there; he only came across it on his desk a week later. Another letter came shortly after that, I knew it would be from Alex because of the handwriting being the same as the first, and then the third came two weeks ago. I thought about telling you, but it was not until the third letter turned up that I realised she must really want to talk to you. I am so sorry I didn't tell you sooner, sweetheart; I wanted to protect you. I thought that reading the letters would bring everything back up, and you seemed to be moving on so well. I am so sorry."

Her eyes glazed with tears; I could tell she was genuinely sorry. A mother only ever wants to protect her daughter, and I tried to remember that. I was speechless.

"How did you even know they were from Alex? Did you read them?"

I asked quizzingly. I could tell instantly by the hand-writing, but my parents wouldn't have known that.

"Your father opened the first one. He saw it was from Alex and put it back. He gave it to me, and I swear to you I didn't read it; the other two are still sealed. I am sure they are very personal and that wouldn't have been fair."

Angered, I responded.

"Oh, but keeping them a secret was fair?"

"You are right; none of it was fair to you."

She placed her hand on mine.

"Why would she even write me a letter? Or should I say three? She has never written to me before. Why now?"

None of it made any sense.

"Maybe it was the best way she knew how to communicate. After all, you did change your number, so even if she wanted to call you, she wouldn't have been able to. Maybe a letter was the next best thing."

It didn't add up. Why a letter? Was she trying to be romantic? Alex had always been a little old-fashioned, terrible with her phone, anything technical she left to Natalie. She preferred the real world, not the world the internet created. The overwhelming urge to know what was in the letters burned inside of me.

"I don't have time for this right now. I need to get to work."

The time on my phone pointing out I should have already left. If Alex wanted to communicate, she could have still sent an email or tried to contact Whitney to get my new number. Either of those things would have made more sense than the three letters that sat before me.

"Do you want me to keep hold of the letters until you get home?"

That would have been the logical thing to do, but I was not thinking logically. Alex had written those letters, the thought of not knowing the contents distressed me deeply. What if I left them and my mom had a change of heart? Maybe she would decide to dispose of them after all. I was being irrational, that is not something she would have done, but any rational thoughts made a swift exit.

"No, it's okay. I think I would like to keep hold of them."

I hugged the letters close to my chest.

"I understand. I am so sorry to have sprung this on you now."

The timing was shabby, but knowing the truth was what mattered.

"Honestly, no hard feelings. I will speak to you later, okay?"

I kissed my mom on the cheek to let her know that all was forgiven. The guilt she felt was punishment enough.

"Okay, darling, I love you."

She bellowed as I swiftly left the kitchen.

"I love you too."

The letters had been strategically stuffed into my work bag, in the pocket to the right that I rarely ever used; they would be safe there, I told myself. The thought of reading them at work had crossed my mind, but if the letters contained what I hoped they would, an explanation, some clarity, some closure, then no doubt it would bring everything back to the surface. The last thing I wanted was to get upset at work.

My day at work, although extremely busy, went extraordinarily slow. Typical really. All I could think about was the letters.

What would they say?

Should I even open them?

Would this give me the closure I needed?

Would I be given an explanation? An apology?

The more I tortured myself with the possibilities of the letters contents, the less I wanted to read them. It had been such a long time since I last spoke to Alex, even longer since I last saw her. There I was, finally starting to move forward, finally starting to feel somewhat human again. Did I want to risk going back to the beginning?

The clock read 6 pm. I had exhausted every option. I could not bring myself to function normally any longer. Grabbing my coat, I ran through a bustling office and straight for the door.

It took me a mere 20 minutes to get home. As I pulled onto the driveway, I could see both my parent's cars were already there. I knew they would be ready with questions about how my day had been, what had I been working on, but my desire to exchange niceties was non-existent. Selfishly.

"Hi honey, how was your day?"

The question came from my dad as soon as I entered the

kitchen. He had recently been working on some private projects from home, and I knew he was generally interested in office life. The enthusiasm I would typically have to entertain such questions had disappeared.

"Hey, Dad. It was average, long; you know how Monday's can be."

He knew them all too well. I hoped he would sense my reluctancy to share in my lame response.

"Do you want to sit down and tell us about it?"

"If you don't mind, I am just going to grab a drink and head up to my room. I am exhausted, and I think I just want to be alone for a while."

My mom smiled sympathetically and glared towards my father to accept my words without pry. She understood why, and I was sure she would soon explain all to my confused father.

"You go ahead, sweetheart; do you want me to plate you up some dinner for later? We are having spaghetti bolognese."

My mom's eyes searched mine as she spoke. She was the one person who had always been able to read me like a book.

"No thanks, Mom. I'm not that hungry. I had a late lunch."

That was a lie, she knew it, and I knew it. She would plate me up some food, whether I wanted it or not. I grabbed a can of soda from the fridge, gave both my parents a reassuring smile and retreated to my bedroom.

The door closed behind me; a sigh of relief left my body. I was finally alone. Eleven hours after I initially found out about the letters. After analysing the situation all day, one thing was as clear as day in my mind. I told myself, *this is your closure*. Would the letters be the final piece of the puzzle? The piece that allowed me to close that chapter of my life for good. There was only one way to find out.

I took out the first letter; it was one A4 sheet of paper. I tried to focus my eyes; tears started to form before I even knew the contents. The sheer sight of my name in her hand-writing brought with it an emotional train. Here goes nothing, I thought.

Kacy,

I know it might seem strange to send a letter, but I saw no other option. I am so unbelievably confused. I tried to call your phone, but it says it is no longer in use. I tried to find you on social media, and you are no longer there? Why?

Why have you stopped contacting me? Did I do something wrong? I keep replaying our last conversations in my head, and I cannot figure out how we got here. Surely, it wasn't because I lost my mobile phone? At least I thought I had. It turns out it had been at Jennifer's house. I must have left it the night that she had the party. I searched for it the next day, and when I couldn't find it, I asked her to message you on social media to tell you I would be getting a new one as soon as possible.
She told me you never replied, which I found strange.

Surprisingly, Jennifer found my phone a few days later, and I had no messages or phone calls from you. I did text Whitney, but she just told me to leave you alone, and then I can only assume she blocked me because I could not contact her after that. Why did she ask me to leave you alone?

I am so confused Kacy. If it's the long-distance that's the problem, surely we can work something out. I will do anything to try and make us work. I miss you so much and I need to hear your voice. I sincerely hope this is one big misunderstanding and that my fears about you finding someone new are entirely untrue.

Please contact me as soon as you get this letter. My number is still the same.
I love you so much, Kace. Don't forget that.
Alex

If I was not already short of answers and explanations, I was even more so after reading the first letter. I re-read the letter three times, each time struggling to make sense of what she was telling me.

Why had I stopped contacting her?

She had lost her phone; was that just an excuse?

Was she just trying to worm her out of the mess she had created?

Maybe she had never intended to get caught out, but that did explain why Jennifer answered her phone when I called. The party also explained the reason she had been at Jennifer's house. To my knowledge, she had planned to go out for drinks with Natalie, but they could have taken a detour. What if Jennifer had wanted me to think that Alex had been there alone? Could she be that calculated? Surely not.

One thing that made absolutely no sense was the timeline of her 'missing' phone. According to Alex, her phone turned up a few days later. Then why had Jennifer answered the phone to me the following day?

The pieces of the puzzle had become even more distorted. Did I believe Alex's innocence and attempt to dig deeper, or did I disregard the letter altogether, putting it down to one last-ditch attempt at protesting her false innocence?

The trust I had formed with Alex had diminished the moment I received her last message. Suddenly, I had reason enough not to trust Jennifer either. Whitney had never mentioned a message from Alex, but like my mom, she always had my best intentions at heart, so that was not surprising.

My breathing became irregular, the pulse in my head beating profusely. My heart was torn, but I had to pull myself together because two more letters remained. The gut-wrenching feeling told me they would not be filled with the answers I was looking for. Had Alex been looking for the same answers?

I carefully peeled away the edges of the second letter. My hands trembled, my composure put to the test. I unravelled two A4 pieces of paper, the second letter visibly lengthier than the first. I stared at the opening line, my eyes glancing towards the end; I wanted the outcome before the suspense destroyed my nervous system. One deep breath, then I delved into the unknown.

Kacy,

No reply? It has been almost two weeks since I last heard anything from you, and I cannot understand what I ever did wrong. I thought we had something special. I thought you loved me in the same uncontrollable, inevitable way that I loved you. I believed that you were my soul mate with all my heart, that even the separation would not harm us, but maybe I was wrong. I just hope you find it within yourself to call me or even text; I will take a text if that is all I can get.

I need some answers from you. Did I do something wrong? Was the long-distance too hard for you? Because it was for me also, but all you had to do was talk to me about it. I keep beating myself up, wondering what I could have done differently. I know that we did not speak as much in the last few days because you were busy with work and I was so busy looking after Rose, but that did not mean for one second that I was not still thinking about you, it would be impossible to stop.

I looked at flights to come and see you so we could figure all this out together in person. That is not a possibility now; I cannot leave Rose. Her health has deteriorated over the past week. This happened before at the beginning, if you remember, so I am hoping she will turn it around this time, but the doctors don't seem so hopeful.

I need you, Kacy. Not hearing from you is breaking my heart every single day. Every day I think about you, I wonder where you are and what you are doing. I just hope that you are happy. If this is it for us, as far as we were supposed to come, then I can accept that, as hard as it may be, I will accept it eventually. I just need to know why. Then if you want me to leave you alone, I will do as you wish.

Can you at least give me that?
Please, Kacy.
I miss you so much.
Alex.

Upon flipping the second piece of paper, I became aware of one solitary sentence scribbled at the bottom of the page, it read.

I will always love you.

The tears streamed uncontrollably, and I let them fall with ease as the sudden realisation that I could have been wrong came to the forefront of my mind. My initial doubts about cutting Alex from my life were correct. My gut had told me it was uncharacteristically harsh. Would I ultimately live to regret it?

My stubborn sense of pride had overtaken every other emotion that appealed to my weaker side. So adamant that I would not let her see me hurt. As I put down the second letter, nausea began. Had I been wrong? Had I jumped to the most damaging conclusion without even waiting for an explanation from Alex? Allowing her the opportunity to convince me otherwise. How had I let that happen?

I was drained, broken down and disorientated. There was one more letter to contend with, and the outcome I feared was a predictable one.

With every ounce of strength I had left, I tore open the last letter and just like clockwork, the tears fell again.

Kacy,

I now, sadly, have my answer. I have wandered Cannon Beach this past week, unable to function, totally lost. Sleep has been a struggle, and the effort it takes to smile seems grand, mainly because a part of me knows that it is really over between us now.
I have re-wrote this letter a dozen times. It started based on anger, followed by resentment and eventually just sadness. I have had a lot of time to think, and I want you to know that as I write this, I have accepted your decision. We can't control everything; I know that now, more than ever.

There will be no harsh exchange of words or bitterness from me because that does not take away from the truth, I love you, and that hasn't changed even if you do not feel the same.
I know that what we had was real for me, which makes saying

goodbye one of the hardest things I have ever had to do.
I have somewhat come to terms with moving on now, but I will miss you deeply. I still hope that you will give me the answers I so desperately need one day, but if not, then I wish you all the best, Kacy.
I am truly sorry things did not work out between us.

Take care of yourself.
Alex.

The last heart-breaking words Alex had written. Words undiscovered, unanswered. The vulnerability in her words crushed me, bringing a heavy weight upon my chest. Alex had poured her heart into three letters, and in my oblivious state, I had responded to none. The unawareness brought with it no relief, only the thoughts of Alex's suffering. My heartbreak now irrelevant somehow. It felt like an unrealistic dream.

Why had I been so quick to tarnish Alex? Her honesty was a trait so dear to her core. She would pride herself upon it. I fought the demons in my own head now. For argument's sake, maybe she had made a mistake; perhaps there was something between her and Jennifer that was undeniable. Why keep up the act? Why pretend she had no idea why we stopped communicating? Was it the guilt?

How was I supposed to make sense of what or who to believe? I had convinced myself wholeheartedly that I had done the right thing. My friends and my family agreed, but all I was left with was a feeling entirely different, one of immense uncertainty.

I had three options. Firstly I could reply to Alex's letter telling her everything I thought had happened, ultimately giving her the explanation she needed. Second, I retrieve her number from Whitney, providing she still had it, and I call her.

Then there was a third option, which was the hardest of them all. I could pretend the three letters did not exist. Instead, I would go back to believing what I initially thought, and my attempts to move on with my life would be unscathed. Or so I told myself.

By the time I had overanalysed every inch of the letters, reading and re-reading, it was too late to decide. I was utterly exhausted. My mind consumed not only thoughts of Alex but also Lara, my parents, and my friends. The next day would bring with it a lot of questions, and I was not sure I would have all the answers.

My first port of call would be to talk with Whitney; she would be able to make sense of the things I could not. At least that is what I told myself, so I could finally fall to sleep.

CHAPTER ELEVEN

"What do you mean you think you got it wrong?"

Whitney's voice screeched down the phone. My first instinct when I woke had been to text her almost immediately. After that, the chance to check my phone and reply had been non-existent. Once it got to lunchtime, I had four missed calls and three messages.

"As I said in the message, it is a hell of a long story. Can I explain everything to you after work? Meet me at my house? I could use your advice."

My lunch break would be cut short by a last-minute meeting that required my presence—no time to talk.

"You cannot, I repeat, cannot, just drop a bombshell like that and then expect me to wait all day, Kacy!!"

I felt sorry for anyone in her presence because the sheer volume of her voice would have been distracting and probably wildly irritating. For me, it was normal.

"I know, and I am sorry. I just really had to get it off my chest this morning. I honestly don't even know where to start, but I promise I will reveal all the detail's later."

Her sigh seriously exaggerated.

"Fine. What time should I come over?"

I was almost positive; she stamped her foot—hilariously.

"I will be finished at six, so anytime around seven. If that is okay with you?"

That gave me enough time to get home, traffic dependant.

"I will be there at seven, not a second later. Just keep it together, okay? Love you."

"I love you too. See you later."

Relief hit when the phone line went silent. The detail had to remain under wraps whilst I was still at work. I could not risk breaking down. Alongside Whitney's mass of missed calls was a text message from Lara. I had barely spoken to her since I found out about the letters, which was unusual for us as of late.

The thought of telling Lara filled me with dread. I needed time to process what had been discovered before discussing it further. I was hopeful that I would have some clarity by the end of the evening.

I composed a message apologising for my lack of communication. I promised I would reveal all the next day. The vague message was less than she deserved, but I did not want to confuse matters further. I knew she would have questions I could not yet answer. Lara was a good woman; I knew she would understand when the time came.

Every second of my day at work had been consumed by the letters. When I arrived home, Whitney had already let herself inside, and she sat cross-legged on my bed, awaiting my arrival.

"Let ourselves in again, did we?"

Whitney yawned for effect.

"Why have a key if you don't use it? You look cute, by the way. Is that a new blouse?"

The blouse was new; she didn't miss a trick.

"Fair point. Do you like it? I wasn't so sure."

I couldn't take the small talk much longer. I was drawn

towards my desk drawer, where I had placed the letters that morning.

"Really cute! Now please explain to me what is going on."

I retrieved the letters from the drawer and lay all three before Whitney.

"What are these?"

She frowned.

"Alex sent them."

She glanced up at me and then back down to the letters.

"What? Why has she written you letters? What do they say?"

I sat at the foot of the bed. There was only one way she would be able to know how I felt. She needed to read them herself.

"The answers to all your questions will be in those letters. They are in order. The one on the left was sent a week after it ended, the next one was a week after that and the last a week after, according to my mom."

Whitney's wide-eyed expression a sign of surprise.

"Why are you only just telling me this now? How long have you had them?"

"My mom was not going to give them to me until she felt too guilty for keeping them a secret. I only read them myself last night."

Whitney gestured furiously towards the letters.

"You have known about these for a full 24 hours, and I am only just seeing them now? You do realise I would have taken the day off work for this?"

Whitney, yet to find a suitable internship, was working at a local newspaper. She had no intention of impressing them, so she genuinely would have called in sick. I nodded regretfully.

"Anyway, I suppose that is beside the point. Do you want me to read them then?"

She held all three letters in her hand suggestively.

"I think that's best. I won't be able to explain it the same. The thought is already making me choke up."

"Okay, give me some time. We will figure all of this out, I promise."

Whitney squeezed my hand reassuringly. What commenced felt like a lifetime of reading. I went to the bathroom to freshen up, changed into some sweats, and even went downstairs to make a snack; when I arrived back upstairs, Whitney was still reading.

"Seriously? I know you are a faster reader than me, so what is taking you so long?"

The suspense was killing me. She rolled her eyes in response.

"Kace, I have read them twice over already. I am just making sure I don't miss any details."

Course she had. After a brief pause, she continued, much to the delight of my eager ears.

"So, let me get this straight…"

Whitney placed the letters down before her and looked directly towards me as she began her interpretation.

"You believed Alex was cheating on you with Jennifer, the phone call she answered, and the fact that Alex never got back to you in the days after made that an almost certainty in your mind. So naturally, with a push from me, you removed her number, you broke off all contact with her, you did what we all thought was the right thing for you to do given the evidence. Let's not forget the *'I am sorry'* text, which sort of sealed the deal. Which she does not seem to mention FYI…"

Whitney had a point; that was the icing on the cake for me. How did she explain that?

"…she either has no idea why you did what you did, or she is an excellent liar. I did not know Alex the way that you did, but I met her enough times to know she loved you, and she was good for you. I was shocked that she would hurt you the way she did, but you were so convinced that as your best friend, I never questioned your judgement, only supported it as I always would."

There was one thing I desperately needed to know from Whitney.

"What did Alex say to you on the message? And why did you keep it from me?"

She sighed. Regretful, it would seem.

"It was really random. I didn't even realise she had my number. She asked me if you were okay and if I would ask you to give her a call. I basically just told her to go away. I thought she was just grovelling, trying to get under your skin. Probably a similar reason to your mom not telling you. I didn't want her to feed you more lies. I can't say I regret it, based on what I knew then, I was doing what I needed to protect my best friend."

I stood up and paced the room. It was too much information in the short space of 24 hours. My emotions overwhelmed me.

"I understand if you are upset with me. It just felt like the right thing to do at the time. You have to remember we assumed she was a cheating, sly, sorry excuse of a woman."

That was true, but ultimately it didn't make it any easier.

"I am just frustrated. If you and my mom had not kept these things a secret from me, then we wouldn't be here. Don't get me wrong, I understand why you did it, and I know that you both just wanted to protect me, but I am also not 16-years-old Whit. I am your best friend, and you should have mentioned it."

My palm wiped the moisture from my forehead, my body burned as I became more irritated, faced with the reality of what I had done.

"I am mainly angry at myself for not giving her the benefit of the doubt. What if this is all my fault?"

Whitney stood from the bed and stopped me in my tracks.

"You are right; I should have told you. It was a bad judgment call, even if I felt it was for the right reasons, but absolutely none of this is your fault. If anything, it's more my fault, and I will accept full responsibility for that."

"How is it your fault?" I questioned.

"I practically forced you into deleting Alex from your life. I don't know if you've noticed, but I can be slightly pushy sometimes. I'll admit it is not my greatest quality."

A crease formed in the corner of my mouth, a somewhat bewildered smile. It was all I could muster.

"Slightly pushy? I haven't noticed at all. It's not your fault either."

Sarcasm came naturally. I used it often to hide my emotional turmoil.

"Very funny! Well, if it's not our fault, and it potentially isn't Alex's either, then I have a funny feeling I know whose fault it is."

I waited for her conclusion.

"Jennifer."

The flawless woman from Alex's past that I knew absolutely nothing about, nor did I care too.

"Why, though? Why would Jennifer go to such lengths?"

Whitney had one hand on either arm as she stood before me. She shook me forcefully, driving me to wake up to the actuality of the situation.

"Is it not obvious? She must like Alex; maybe she was jealous because she had a girlfriend. She was presented with an opportunity to make it seem like she and Alex were more than friends, and she took it."

It was speculation, but it did make sense.

"Do you think she kept her phone from her on purpose? And maybe she sent the last text message?"

Whitney raised her eyebrows as if to say, *'you are kidding, right'* I was clearly too naive. I did not want to believe that someone could be so malicious and unkind.

"You are damn right I think that's what happened. You know Jennifer had that phone because she answered it, but Alex tells you in the letter that she didn't get it back until days later."

That made Jennifer the prime suspect.

"Jennifer knew you would have assumed the worse by then. She is extremely vindictive if that's the case. The whole plan worked perfectly in her favour."

It was hard to believe, if true, she was relentless and somewhat unstable.

"What am I going to do, Whit? If I give Alex the benefit of the doubt. How will I ever fix this? It has been almost five weeks since I last spoke to her. Where do I even start?"

I slumped on the bed, head in hands, utter disbelief. Whitney instantly consoled me.

"Listen, Alex is not just anyone. She is potentially the love of your life. I think you need answers, Kace. I think you need to talk to her about how it all went wrong from your perspective, explain to her everything you felt, your reasonings for doing what you did. You need to explain your theories about Jennifer and see what her reaction is. I know this is difficult for you, but you have a chance to make it right."

I asked myself, where do I even begin with something like that.

"Is a phone call going to achieve that? I would probably just choke up as soon as I heard her voice. Besides, I highly doubt she even wants to speak to me anymore."

A lightbulb moment occurred for Whitney as she lunged

from the bed.

"I have a better idea! You go and see her in person. Like literally fly out to Oregon and see her face to face. You're right something like this should not be done over the phone, and it would also be incredibly romantic, and I am all for that."

I looked at her in utter disbelief.

"What? That's crazy! I mean, even if I wanted to, I don't have time to go to Oregon Whit."

Here comes the counter-argument to every excuse I could conjure up—my exact thoughts.

"Course you do. You said yourself you could do with a long weekend. So, take one, I am just spitballing here, but you could literally fly out on Thursday night and come back Saturday or Sunday. It would be brief, but it would give you the chance to talk things through, see if you can figure all this out."

She made it seem so straight forward, but she possessed characteristics that thrived on the environment I found myself in. I was realistic and cautious, maybe too much so.

"Thursday is literally two days away; that is incredibly short notice. I don't work somewhere that just lets me do as I please."

"You know they owe you. You have gone above and beyond since you started there. You could turn around tomorrow and ask them for a day off. If it is something you really wanted, you could do it. So, how much do you want it?"

That was a fully loaded question.

"I want her. I have never not wanted her…but what if I get there and she doesn't want to see me anymore? It would destroy me, Whitney."

Another one of Whitney's classic faces involved a slight pout of the lips, a crease of the forehead and a wrinkle of the nose. It basically said, *'Are you for real?'* I was well acquainted with that face.

"Honestly, if you weren't my best friend and I didn't know how incredibly bright you are, I would think you were really stupid! Alex loves you, Kacy! If that is not completely obvious from those letters, then I don't know what is. Feelings like that don't just disappear."

Charming.

"I am being stupid, aren't I? Okay, but if I do go. I can't go alone."

There was absolutely no way I would make it to the airport on my own. My nerves would get the better of me, that I knew for sure. There was no hesitation in Whitney's response.

"Say no more. I am there." She grinned.

"What about work? I can't ask you to drop everything to come on some mad adventure with me."

There was that look again.

"You didn't ask me to, I insist. Work can wait; they do not control my life. They are lucky to even have me working there."

Whitney gave me her most convincing smile. I was so grateful as always to have her support. She immediately dialled a number on her cell phone.

"Jordan, it's Whitney. Yeah, so about this Friday, I need to take the day off. I know. Yeah. I know, but it is crucial. I will. Okay great. Thank you. Bye."

Just like that, she no longer had to work. It must be nice to be that influential, I thought.

"Done. Now whilst you speak to your boss, I am going to look at some flights for Thursday night."

It was all moving extremely fast.

"What would I do without you?"

She shrugged her shoulders.

"Honestly? I really don't know. You'd be living a very dull, monotonous life probably."

Whitney winked before bounding over to the computer in the corner of my room. She was made for moments like that; within minutes, I knew she would have a flight booked, and the plans would be cemented in concrete, leaving me no choice but to face my problems head-on.

After speaking briefly with my boss, I had secured Friday off. I told him it was an emergency, and I would rather not discuss it. There was a real understanding in his voice and concern that I assured was not necessary; I would reveal all eventually if he so wished to know. I heard the printer start up, and Whitney was stood before me again with two boarding passes, just like magic.

"All done. Two flights to Oregon for Thursday night, we fly out at 6.35 pm."

I gave her the biggest hug I could fathom.

"Thank you so much Whit. I honestly would not be able to do this without you."

The price had seemed irrelevant, considering the circumstances—an afterthought.

"Oh god, how much do I owe you?"

"Please, my dad has enough air miles to fly us around the world four times over. I have got this one covered."

She never ceased to amaze me.

"You are the best, do you know that?"

"I have been told once or twice. Shall we start planning?"

That was a no brainer; I had a lot to consider. I hugged her again, finally letting the emotion overcome me. Tears quickly formed, and I knew they would not be the last.

"Let's do it."

It was Tuesday, and I now had two whole days to wait until I could fly out and see Alex. Two full days to prepare exactly what I would say. I only had one chance to get it right, that is, if she was even willing to see me in the first place. I had almost immediately begun to think I was in the wrong. I had dropped all previous assumptions upon reading the letters. I went with my gut feeling as I always did. I weighed up every shred of evidence and concluded that frustratingly there was no way of truly knowing until I spoke to Alex in person. Whitney was right; it was easy to lie over text, it was easy to lie in a letter or even over the phone, but face to face was always so much harder. If the signs were there, I would see them.

We spent the rest of the evening making the necessary travel arrangements. There were more than enough places to stay in Cannon Beach, Oregon. We decided upon a nice privately run bed and breakfast called the Lighthouse Inn; it was perfect for what we wanted. The flight time to Oregon was roughly five hours, which meant we would arrive close to midnight on Thursday evening, which suited us both fine. It meant we could get some sleep before I ventured fully into the unknown.

The next morning, I had a discussion with my parents. There had been minimal conversation between us since receiving the letters. I was not blaming them; I frankly had not been ready to discuss it. I needed to explain what the letters meant as best I could. They deserved to know what was going on with their only daughter, and if anything to put my mother's mind at ease, she was a worrier.

"Morning, sweetheart. How are you feeling today?"

Michelle gave me her award-winning smile as I entered the kitchen.

"Morning, Mom, I am okay. Late-night though, I am certainly feeling it this morning."

Anything less than seven solid hours of sleep should be a crime.

"I thought I didn't hear Whitney leave. What time did you get to sleep?"

Michelle began to punch buttons on the coffee machine. Mind-reader.

"No, she left just after midnight. I think I managed to get to sleep around 2 am."

It was 7 am, and coffee would be the only thing to save me.

"Did you discuss the letters?"

I could tell she felt uncomfortable asking. Even with her back turned, she stiffened, awaiting my response.

"Yes, for the most part. It kind of took a crazy turn after that. There is something I need to tell you."

She placed the cappuccino before me; it smelt absolutely divine.

"What is it, sweety?"

"The letters did shed some light on a few things. I may have been wrong; I may have even slightly overreacted to the whole situation. I can't be 100% sure, but I won't know until I get some answers from Alex. Which brings me to the next part."

I took a sip of my coffee, bliss. I was trying to anticipate her reaction.

"I am flying out to Oregon on Thursday night to get some answers. Whitney is going to come with me."

She was surprised, somewhat sceptical.

"That was unexpected. I am assuming you have spoken with Alex?"

"Not quite."

Michelle Sullivan raised a suspicious eyebrow, urging me to continue.

"I figured a phone call or an email would not suffice this time."

"Why does this have Whitney Sawyer written all over it?"

Was it that obvious I did not act so spontaneously without my side-kick?

"Kacy, are you sure you are doing the right thing?"

Truth be told, I had no idea.

"Honestly, I don't know what is the best thing to do right now. This is all new information to me."

She walked around the breakfast bar and placed her hand on my shoulder.

"You were so certain about what happened with you and Alex. Are you sure you made a mistake? I don't want you going all the way out there and realising what you already suspected."

I couldn't be 100% sure about anything.

"I know it sounds crazy, but if there is a chance I can fix this, I have to try at least, right? I know you probably think it's a long shot, but I am so over hating her; I don't want to hate her anymore, Mom."

Etched upon my mom's face was sympathy. She brushed the hair lovingly from my eyes before she spoke.

"I will support you in whatever you choose to do; you know that. You will always be my baby girl, and I will never stop worrying about you, but you are a woman now, and I trust your judgment. Whatever happens this weekend, it is what is meant to happen; remember that."

She did not enquire any more. I was sure she had a million questions, but she refrained from asking. It was something I had to do on my own, for myself, for my peace of mind.

CHAPTER TWELVE

JOURNAL ENTRY 26/11/2010

I now know what I need to do. I hope with all my heart that everything works out for the best, but I will not sit here and write about how I want to get Alex back and live happily ever after. I am a realist, and things will work out the way they are supposed to, even if that means me and Alex are not meant to find our way back to each other.

My mom is a true believer in fate and destiny, I guess I am too in some ways, but I believe that I make my own choices. I chose to love Alex; I decided to leave Alex, and now I choose to fly to Oregon to get her back. These are all my choices, but I do like to think that fate & destiny had a little bit to do with how we met and how we will meet again.

I just got off the phone with Whitney; we fly out to Oregon tomorrow. The day has finally arrived. I am incredibly nervous, mainly because I don't know what to expect. I have not dwelled too much on the possibility that she might ignore me completely, which is altogether possible.

Alex is an understanding person, but I may have overstepped the mark slightly. Anyway, that is enough speculating from me; my mind hurts with the number of times I keep changing it. I need to talk to Lara before I forget. I will do that now.

Lara Manning was not a person you easily forgot about. The time we spent together had not been in vain. I cared for her, and I always would. Despite my lack of communication, she did not bombard me or get upset. Instead, she waited patiently for me to check in when I was ready. Lara was that person, the one who managed to be totally selfless and kind whilst being beautiful both inside and out. Finding a person like that was rare. There were very few genuine souls in the world, and that brought a tear to my eye. Whatever we had become in recent weeks, there was one thing I was sure of; I wanted her to be a part of my life.

When I searched deep within my soul, one thing was unmistakable; I loved Lara. I just loved Alex differently. Inevitably some might have said. People would not understand; if asked to explain, I don't think I would have been able to. I do not believe you can be genuinely in love with two people at once, but I think you can love two people in a different capacity at the same time.

Sometimes another human being comes into your life, and it is apparent on some level that you belong together, whether that is as lovers, friends or as something entirely different. That is how I felt about Lara. We just worked, we understand one another, we were comfortable beyond belief in one another's presence. The few weeks we had spent together brought back the realisation that we had a bond that would never disappear.

It was 9 pm, and I knew there was a phone call I had to make. I owed her an explanation.

"Hey, Kace! Finally, you call!"

She was chipper despite the lack of contact on my end.

"Lara, I am so sorry. I understand if you want to yell at me, swear at me, tell me I am a horrible person. I'm totally prepared for it."

She laughed, and the sound was like music to my ears.

"You don't need to apologise; I figured you needed some space. I know you wouldn't blow me off unless there was a pretty good reason, so I trusted that."

How could I not love her?

"My mind has been all over the place lately. Are you okay?"

"You know me; I am perfectly fine. I have done absolutely nothing of interest since I last saw you, so I will not bore you with it. The real question is…are you okay?"

She was the most understanding person in the world, that made the guilt of ignoring her even worse.

"Not really. I don't even know where to start."

"Then start at the top. You can tell me anything, Kace, anything at all."

I wanted to be able to tell her everything; the difficult part was how to put it. How do you feel comfortable pouring your heart out to someone you had feelings for when it wasn't about them?

"Basically, a few days ago, my mom gave me some letters, three all together, they were from Alex. I struggled at first to know what to make of them. I still am really struggling with it."

I took a deep breath; the line remained silent. I was waiting for a response, anything at all.

"Okay, so what did the letters say?"

It felt like a deja vu moment. Reluctantly there I was again, explaining as much as I could understand. I went ahead and relayed all three letters' contents, as much as I felt she needed to know. Once I finished, Lara's reply was instantaneous.

"That is a lot to process. Do you believe everything she said? You know her better than I do, so I will trust your instincts."

The golden question, again.

"I think so. I have been back and forth a million times in my head. Whitney has seen the letters too, and she agrees. I didn't know how to reach out to you about it. It's all so complicated, and I didn't want to put that on you and make you feel uncomfortable in any way."

There was a pause on the line. Hesitation maybe.

"You could have told me. We both agreed for this to be casual. We both consented to this, knowing that it may be complicated down the line, so don't worry about me. I would much rather you keep me in the loop."

"I do worry about you though. I care about you Lara. I would never want to hurt you."

"You won't hurt me, I promise."

There was a momentary pause.

"If you don't mind me asking…now you have this information…what are you going to do?"

The next part was what I feared the most in terms of a response.

"I made a split second decision after me and Whitney spoke about the letters. I am flying out to Oregon tomorrow to see her. I could not see another way."

The line went entirely silent.

"Oh…okay."

I cut her off immediately to explain.

"It's just something I need to do; I hope you understand that. I need to know what happened to move forward. I just want you to know that what has been happening with us, it meant something to me. You mean something to me. I can't explain it; this is just something I have to do. I can't help it."

There was no hint of sadness in her voice when she spoke again, only encouraging words.

"What I was going to say was, I think you are doing the right thing. I know you are not trying to hurt me Kace, and you haven't. If it turns out that Alex is not the bad guy, then I know that any future with us is doubtful, but I am okay with that. This was fun while it lasted, but I would like to think that aside from the romantic connection, we formed a strong friendship that can go beyond that. I am here for you if you need me, no matter what. There will be no hard feelings; I promise you that."

I had to stop myself from crying, not because I was sad, but because I knew how amazing Lara was, she had such a kind heart. A part of me felt at a loss that I had not kept her in my life, the absence of three years too long to comprehend, she had fast become one of the best people I knew.

"Lara, you are the best, and I am so unbelievably thankful that we found each other again. If you think I am letting you get away that easy, then you are crazy. You will be my friend for life now, whether you like it or not."

I tried to joke, holding back the tears.

"I like the sound of that Kace. Just promise me one thing?"

"Anything."

"Don't feel like you have to keep things from me; you can tell me anything. I only want what is best for you, you are a great girl, and you deserve that."

The sincerity was lost on the next part.

"Also, if you and Alex don't work out, then you call me up because I will be here waiting for that second chance. If she doesn't jump at the chance to have you back, then she is absolutely insane."

We laughed naturally. Despite the seriousness of the conversation, Lara would always try to lighten the mood. Having her in my corner to navigate through life was a blessing. I hoped with all my heart we could make it work. My response surprised us both.

"I love you, Lara."

As if I were simply saying hello, the words left my mouth with ease. Her response, as apparent and true, ended our conversation.

"I love you too Kace. Now go get your girl. Call me when you're back?"

"You bet."

It was 4 pm on Thursday; my previous night's sleep had been disturbed beyond belief. I saw every hour of my alarm clock, much to my agitation. The plan was to pick Whitney up at 4.30 pm and head straight to the airport, which would give us enough time to check-in and grab some dinner before the flight. The flight I surprisingly looked forward to in the hope that I would be able to catch up on some well-needed beauty sleep.

There had only been business class seats available on the day we booked, but I was grateful for the extra legroom and reclining seats. I guess I had Whitney's dad to thank for that. Everything ran smoothly from arriving at the pre-paid car park to check-in to security and passport control. It was plain sailing, no body searches, and no mile-long queues. It was my lucky day.

The woman behind the register at the coffee counter even struck up a conversation to which afterwards she stated that the coffee was on her. My confidence boosted immediately, running off no more than four hours of sleep, dressed from head to toe in my comfy clothes with my hair scraped back, and I still managed to get a free coffee. Things were looking up.

"Look at you with that grin; I guess coffee girl doesn't think you look bad at all. Now you can stop moaning."

Whitney walked off, chuckling to herself, making it more

than evident to the cashier that we were blatantly talking about her. I was trying my best to stop overanalysing everything. I knew having Whitney with me would take my mind off most things, I started to think of it as a girly weekend away, and if I happened to bump into Alex whilst I was there, well, I would deal with that at the time. It was the only way I could keep myself calm.

The flight went smoothly. The drinks frequently came, which helped me get the three hours' sleep I craved. There were no screaming children in business class, and that I was thankful for. Whitney, a frequent flyer, was slightly more prepared than I was. The contents of a small green make-up bag consisted of one set of earplugs, some hard-boiled sweets, lip balm and a gorgeous super soft cotton eye mask.

An hour before landing and I was abruptly awakened from my sleep by some extreme turbulence. Whitney was already perfectly groomed and reading the latest gossip magazines.

"Hey, sleepyhead."

"How long was I out?"

I gripped the armrest as I propped myself up—more turbulence.

"Probably two hours. You are cute when you sleep."

I rolled my eyes and pointed directly to the birds' nest on my head. The reflection in the monitor in front made me instantly aware I looked anything but cute.

"What is cute about this?"

I tried to fix it to no avail. Whitney laughed and returned to the gossip column she was so absorbed in.

"This turbulence is horrible."

My flying partner was utterly unphased.

"This is nothing. It has been going on for about 15 minutes; I am surprised you have only just woken up. Did I tell you about the time I thought I was going to die?"

It was diabolical timing, but I knew she would tell me anyway.

"That depends because you have nearly died on several occasions, so what are we referring too."

I searched aimlessly for my bottle of water.

"I flew to Thailand with my family when I was about 16; honestly, it was the first real time I had experienced turbulence. It was so bad. There was a storm outside; we had to circle for almost an hour before we could land. The plane was shaking; even my dad was scared, I could tell in his face. Since that experience, no turbulence has been half as bad, so it doesn't even bother me. Every cloud, I suppose."

Well, I would look to Whitney to gage my reaction in future, I thought. If she was scared, I should be petrified.

"The thought is making me feel anxious. Do you know how far away we are?"

A change of subject eased the tension.

"The captain came on not too long ago, about 55 minutes, I think, probably more like 45 now. Are you nervous?"

Nervous was an understatement.

"When I think about it, I want to throw up, so yes, I guess you could say I am a little nervous."

She placed her magazine reluctantly back in her bag, her full attention aimed towards me.

"That is natural, Kace. If you didn't feel nervous, I would be asking you why you are even going."

She had a point.

"I suppose you are right. If I feel like throwing up when going for a job interview, then surely, I should feel worse when going to secretly confront the woman I am in love with, who I haven't seen for four months."

The nausea was even worse when I said it out loud. What was I thinking?

"Well yeah, when you put it like that. So, you are still in love with her?"

That was a simple answer.

"I never stopped being in love with her. I tried, but it was impossible."

She smiled and offered me a hard mint.

"Then it's a good thing we have come all this way. Here have a mint."

"Does my breath smell?"

I pretended to look offended.

"It's for the decent you idiot. Now that you say it, though, maybe you could use another."

I snatched the mint.

"Give me that."

"So, what is the plan of action once we land?"

I wish I knew.

"I was kind of just hoping you would take care of absolutely everything."

She considered it.

"Normally, yes, but I draw the line at talking to Alex for you. I really think that is something you need to do yourself."

"Really? Damn."

Whitney's carefree approach helped me remain calm. Whitney often took control of situations when I struggled to make a decision; it was one of those times.

"I think we need to grab a taxi to the B&B, check-in and get some sleep. Tomorrow will be a long day. We can try and figure out where Alex is staying. You said you had the address, right?"

I pulled my diary from my bag, and there on the contacts page was her Cannon Beach address.

"She gave it to me when she moved, in case of an emergency. This counts, right?"

"Oh, 100%."

The security and passport control in Oregon was just as smooth as North Carolina; it seemed someone was looking down on me. I hoped the good fortune would continue. We did not need to wait for our baggage as we only had hand luggage for the short stay. All in all, it took a quick 20 minutes to get through the airport. The weather was relatively mild, with no rain and the wind minimal. A line of 20 cabs awaited as we left the airport, we jumped in the first one available to us.

"Hi, Cannon Beach please, The Lighthouse Inn."

"Certainly, ladies. Make yourself comfortable. It will be about 30 minutes."

Said the cheerful cab driver; he was around 50 years old and very handsome.

"Thank you."

Whitney and I said in unison. The cab driver didn't have much to say on the journey, which I was thankful for, me and Whitney had so much to talk about that the 30 minutes flew by. We pulled up outside the Lighthouse Inn at around 1 am; it looked beautiful from the outside, and the exterior was primarily wooden, which added so much character. Lights surrounded the whole B&B, so much so that it illuminated the night sky. The suites across the front all had a balcony that overlooked the beach. It was even better than I expected it to be.

We were promptly shown to our room on arrival. The Queen suite happened to be the only one available at such short notice. Everything from the traditional red décor, to the flat-screen TV, to the picturesque flower-filled balcony, was all so clean and beautifully presented. Instantly I felt it was a place I would love to come to again. I dropped my carry on at the door and sprawled out across the bed, comfort was critical, and it didn't disappoint. We prepared for bed, knowing the next day would bring with it so much uncertainty.

The next morning Whitney placed the telephone back in its cradle after a quick conversation with the receptionist.

"They are going to call us a cab; she said it would be about ten minutes. Are you nearly ready to head out?"

"As ready as I will ever be."

We discussed going to a café in town first. I would need a stronger coffee than the B&B could provide. It only took a short five-minute cab drive into the small town. On the surface, it looked pleasant. You could tell it was a close-knit community, something that was familiar to me from when I lived in Hyde County. There was an atmosphere in a small town that was difficult to describe to other's if you had never lived in one. There is an intimacy about it, a peaceful calm, a local café where everyone is known by name, a local bar where everyone runs up a tab and is trusted to pay, the type of place if your dog went missing, the whole community would be out looking for it. It is nice, but also on the reverse, a very invasive way to live.

Choosing the perfect place to grab something to eat was a task. For a small town, there was a steady stream of coffee shops and cafés; every other shop front posed a new option for us both. After walking for a minute or two, we settled on a small, family-run café called Susan's Café. Whitney, like me, was a huge fan of waffles for breakfast, so the first thing on the menu she ordered instantly. I, on the other hand, was not sure I could stomach anything.

"How about we share it then? You need to eat something, Kace."

The oatmeal waffle delight did look appealing.

"Maybe I could squeeze in a bite or two."

The conversation began to flow whilst we ate. It was by far the most amazing waffle I had ever tried, such a beautiful presentation with an array of fruits topped off with whipped cream and chocolate sauce. Usually, I would have been in absolute heaven, but the nausea was not easing off.

"Well, for someone who didn't want any of the waffle, the chocolate sauce on your lip says otherwise."

Whitney howled at my expense.

"Are you kidding? How long has that been there?"

I wiped ferociously at my lip.

"Only a few minutes. I thought about allowing you to walk out of here like that, but I love you too much to do that to you."

I gave her my best scowl.

"I would have killed you!!"

If the chair she was perched upon didn't have armrests, I would have expected to see her rolling on the floor.

"Yeah yeah! So are you almost ready to go?"

Hardly.

"No, quite the opposite, but we are here now. The more I think about just turning up on her doorstep, the more nervous I get. I keep trying to imagine what her reaction is going to be"

My heart would not stop beating out of my chest.

"I know. No amount of role-playing will prepare you for that moment, so just go with the flow Kace. I can go back to the hotel if you like or come along; it is completely up to you. Although I don't aspire to be the third wheel."

The last sip of coffee touched my lips. It was time.

"I think it's something I need to do on my own, isn't it?"

She smiled as we gathered our things.

"I agree."

Over breakfast, we had discovered the place Alex currently lived was within walking distance of the café. We figured out the direction roughly; it would only take ten minutes, which would give me enough time to think about my approach.

"Why don't you hang around town? There seems to be plenty of shops you could explore. Surely that is better than going back to the hotel."

Whitney's eyes lit up; she was the ultimate queen of shopping.

"Good idea. Did you see that beautiful boutique on the way in? The dress in the window was to die for. You've twisted my arm. You take your time. I'm sure there are enough shops here to keep me busy for a few hours."

I felt guilty leaving Whitney behind, but it was to be expected. We had gone for one reason, and she knew that.

"Thank you for being so understanding and just being here with me. I know I have said it ten times already, but you are the best."

We finished up at the café and made our way back onto the main street. The tourist element was bearable, nothing like the hustle and bustle I had expected. I could see almost immediately why Rose loved the place so much and why Alex had settled there just fine. I walked Whitney back towards the boutique and gave her a quick hug goodbye before setting off in the opposite direction.

"Good luck Kace. Keep me updated."

"I will do. See you later. Love you."

As I wandered down the half-empty street, I contemplated turning around on more than one occasion, but what my heart wanted always prevailed and what it wanted was Alex. That I knew with every inch of my being, so I owed it to myself to try.

How the tides had changed since earlier that week, the girl I loved, the girl I had fallen so deeply in love with, had hurt me in a way I had never been hurt before. My heart had been broken into what felt like a million tiny pieces. I felt as though piecing them back together was impossible. I had clinched onto every hope when I read the letters because I still was not over her. She had touched my soul in such a way that I could not physically nor mentally remove her from it.

What would I do if everything I had come to believe was true? If the newfound hope I had was suddenly shattered, that's when reality would surely hit me like a ton of bricks, but that was a chance I was willing to take. My only thought - I had not come this far to turn back now.

Then I saw her.

CHAPTER THIRTEEN

Have you ever felt everything and nothing all at the same time? It is an indescribable experience. To feel every crack of your heart, but at the same time feel so numb that you are not even sure it is really happening. To hold little pockets of hope and then suddenly have each one of them ripped from your grasp as though they never existed.

What I saw before me was a vivid, intense realisation. The emotions I had hidden away due to a newfound hope flooded back eagerly. They had been waiting, silently at bay, for their moment to reappear. My emotions took control; I watched as though I was detached from my body with no ability to move. My overriding thought was one of sheer distress, as though she was still mine. Except she was not mine, she did not stand beside me anymore, she stood beside her, a dream gone wrong. I had foolishly placed too much faith in something I could not control.

Seconds passed, my body was completely frozen to the ground, unable to move in any shape or form. Alex was right in front of me, as beautiful as I remembered. Only she was not alone. Their hands intertwined, they strolled down the street as though they had no care in the world. Alex and Jennifer. My worst nightmare.

I had been dead-on all along. I wanted to run as far away from Cannon Beach as humanly possible. My legs refused to move, giving up just as my heart did. I had no choice but to observe the ultimate betrayal playing out before my eyes like a surreal, slow-motion movie, what I would have given to wake up.

What I found unconventional was the way Alex held Jennifer at a distance, unhappy it would seem, to be showing such public displays of affection. Did I hope that was the case? It was a picture far different from the way we used to be together. They looked to be shopping, and I watched as they entered a small boutique, five stores down from where I stood.

The boutique looked familiar, the dress in the display window in particular. Then it struck me that was the boutique Whitney had been so eager to enter only ten minutes earlier. How was this happening to me? My mind boggled. I wanted nothing more than to turn and leave, but if Alex saw Whitney, she would know I was there too. I had to pull myself together.

My first instinct was to call Whitney and tell her to leave the boutique. I fumbled around in my pocket for my phone and immediately hit the first number on speed dial.

"Hey Kace, everything okay?"

Relief.

"Whitney, you need to get out of that boutique, like right now."

"What are you talking about? What's wrong?"

Make sense, I told myself. I started pacing.

"Alex has just entered with Jennifer; I will explain later, but we need to leave."

Her voice went up several decibels, almost matching my own.

"What? Okay, I am just in the changing room trying on a dress. How am I supposed to get around them? This place isn't exactly huge."

Whitney's voice lowered to just above a whisper when she realised they would be able to hear her every word.

"Oh god!! You will have to wait in the changing room until their gone then. Can you do that?"

"Kace, there is only one changing room in here, and a woman wanted to use it after me... we need a plan B."

Hysteria would soon take over.

"This is not how this was supposed to play out. Just get out of there, please. Maybe if they see you, just say you have taken a trip with your mom. You have a great poker face; put it to good use."

If it were plausible at that moment for the world to open and swallow me whole, I would have been grateful. I did not wish to live through the ordeal any longer. Stealthily, I tracked back slightly towards the boutique and watched from behind a large oak tree. Terribly covert. My view was distorted from across the street. The suns glare bounced back off the windows, making it impossible to give Whitney any guidance on their whereabouts inside the store.

"Kace, I'm going to go because I can't concentrate with you breathing down my ear. I will be out soon."

The line went dead; she had to get out unseen. The last thing I wanted or needed was a confrontation with Alex and Jennifer. I had been correct with my assumptions all along, and the worse thing was, my optimism had given me hope. I wanted to believe everything she wrote in those letters, and I did. Gullible Kacy Sullivan, as always.

My mind pondered as I awaited Whitney's great escape. If Alex saw me now, would she tell me she had made a mistake or had I been just as dispensable to her as anyone else? With every agonising second that passed, my mind tortured me. Whitney eventually came bounding out of the boutique. My heart halted until I realised nobody was following her; she did it. I signalled for her to join me across the street, trying not to slip out from behind my tree trunk disguise.

"Please tell me you got away without them seeing you?"

"Not quite."

Whitney took a moment to catch her breath.

"What do you mean, not quite?"

The sheer panic in my voice was evident.

"Alex saw me, well actually, Jennifer turned just as I was passing by, and I bumped into her. Alex turned to see me; she didn't move or say anything. I didn't know what to say, so I just said *'Sorry'*, and I practically ran from the shop."

Just when I thought it could not get any worse.

"Oh god, this is bad. Alex is obviously going to think that I am here with you. Why else would you be in Cannon Beach."

I ushered Whitney further down the tree-lined street. I could not stand within such close proximity to Alex anymore.

"I'm sorry, Kace. I tried so hard to get out of there, and if it wasn't for that devil of a woman."

Whitney looked back towards the boutique to see if anyone had followed.

"What happened to the whole I am on vacation with my mom story we spoke about?"

"Oh, come on, we both know she wouldn't buy it. Besides, I didn't want to stick around. If I got talking to her, I was afraid I might say something I would regret."

A little further on, I peered back around the corner as we turned onto a different street. Alex and Jennifer promptly left the boutique, the handholding had stopped, and they looked to be having a heated conversation. Even the brief sight of the back of Alex left me paralysed.

"This could not have gone any worse. Can we just head back to the room? I can't think straight."

Whitney nodded in agreement.

We arrived back at the B&B promptly, which I was thankful for. No sooner than my foot entering the room did the questions begin.

"You still haven't explained what all that was about?"

"What's there to explain? They are clearly together now." Whitney tried to reason.

"Could they not just be there as friends? Not to defend Alex, but you never know."

In my panic, I had missed out the most vital piece of information.

"No, I saw them, clear as day, walking down the street hand in hand."

Her face dropped immediately.

"Oh. I am so sorry Kace. Do you think she saw you? I bet she would feel like an awful person if she knew you were here."

I didn't want her to know. I had been embarrassed enough for one day.

"I don't think she did. What was I thinking, Whit? Flying five hours to speak to someone who completely broke my heart."

Whitney sat beside me and held my hand in hers.

"It is her loss babe. Don't you ever forget that."

She brushed away the solitary tear that rolled down my cheek.

"On a lighter note, did you see what Jennifer was wearing? I don't like her or her fashion sense."

I laughed through the pain; staying strong proved difficult.

"She is not worth your tears, she will realise deep down what she has lost, and she will be kicking herself for the rest of her life. Whilst she is living a life of misery, you will move on to bigger and better things with some gorgeous girl that will make you forget all about Alex Dawson. Don't ever forget just how beautiful, kind, smart and funny you are. You even give me a run for my money."

She nudged me playfully before continuing.

"I will give you time to recover because I know this is hurting you, but when you are ready, we will find you someone worthy. Hey, there is always Lara; she seems to be stepping up to the plate lately. Don't rule her out, will you."

"Thanks, Whit. I love you."

"Love you too, baby girl."

The afternoon passed by sluggishly. We took full advantage of the free room service for a late lunch and dessert before likewise eyeing up the dinner menu. The thought of leaving our room filled me with anxiety. The whereabouts of Alex were unknown to me, and the thought of bumping into her was not comprehendible. I had to avoid that at all costs.

It was 5 pm, only another 24 hours of anguish before we could finally get our fight back to Raleigh. The possibility of switching to an earlier flight had diminished quickly after speaking with the airline. There was no other choice but to binge watch daytime TV and order room service.

On my return from the kitchenette, glass of water in hand, to my surprise, the phone started ringing. I assumed it must be the reception.

"Hello."

"Hello Miss Sullivan, your guest is here at reception. Would you like me to send them up to your room?"

My guest? Panic.

"I'm sorry, but I am not expecting a guest. Could you ask them who it is, please?"

Whitney entered the room; her quizzing eyes looked at the

receiver then back at me.

"The ladies name is Alex Dawson. She has asked if you would kindly join her in the lobby. Would you prefer me to decline?"

I slammed the phone back down as I slumped onto the bed. The woman at reception would assume I was obnoxious, but her opinion of me was irrelevant at that moment. I could not breathe; how did she know I was there.

"Whitney, it's Alex. She's waiting in the lobby; she wants to see me."

Whitney instinctively stomped towards the door.

"Shall I go and tell her to leave?"

She would not be afraid to accost Alex, which I was sure of, but the last thing I wanted was a confrontation on my behalf.

"I think I need to face her, don't I?"

I needed reassurance.

"You do whatever you are comfortable with."

I was not at all comfortable with anything that involved Alex at that present time, but what choice did I have?

"I don't want to cower away like some scared, heartbroken, little girl. She knows I am here; I cannot give her the satisfaction of knowing I am hurting. I refuse to give her that."

Whitney clenched her fist in solidarity.

"That's my girl; you do not back down, and do not let her see you cry. You go down there confidently and tell her she has made the biggest mistake she will ever make and then walk away with your head held high."

That was my intention exactly. Luckily for me, I hadn't taken my make up off, so I gave myself a quick check over in the mirror, added a touch of hairspray and a squirt of my favourite perfume before heading to the door. Whether she had broken my heart or not, I still wanted her to find me attractive.

"Good luck." Whitney called out.

I had never felt my heart pound so profoundly in my chest. I could feel every thud like it would explode at any moment. My reaction upon seeing her would be a surprise to myself as well as her. How do you feel love, hatred, joy, and heartbreak all at the same time? I had to face what had haunted me so powerfully over the previous five weeks. I walked the long corridor to the lobby; each side decorated so loudly with vibrant orange and red designs. Vases of flowers were placed on solid wood stands every few metres. I tried to look everywhere but forward. I took a deep breath as I urged my legs to take the last few strides.

Alex was the first thing I saw in a noticeably quiet room, perched by the window with her phone in hand. As I got within a few paces, she glanced up, startled. She jumped up from her seat and dropped her phone. That did not bother her though, she left it lying on the floor as she stared at me. Our eyes locked, a trance-like state overcame us both. There she was, as perfectly groomed as ever. She had made an almighty effort, and it had not gone unnoticed.

Had she done that to taunt me? Look at what you once had. No, surely not, even I did not believe she could be so cruel. She studied all of me from head to toe, blatantly making me incredibly nervous. After what felt like a lifetime, she finally broke the silence.

CHAPTER FOURTEEN

"I didn't think you would come down. I was willing to wait here all night if that's what it took."

There was no emotion escaping the vacant look I possessed. I was not sure how long I would be able to keep up the act.

"How did you know I was here?"

"It's a small town, Kace. There are only so many places you could be, so I tried them all."

I should have known it would not have been difficult. Small towns. No place to hide. The familiar way in which she called me *'Kace'* sent a shiver through my entire body.

"What do you want, Alex?"

The surprise caused by my abrupt response was obvious. "When I saw Whitney, I assumed you would be here with her. Why are you here Kacy? Did you come to see me?"

To the point, she had not changed.

"Do not flatter yourself, Alex."

The hurt flashed across her face; instantly, I felt guilty.

"I'm sorry, I just assumed with you being here, of all places…" She paused. "Why didn't you call me or write me back?"

The last part was a plea; she was desperate to know—the audacity.

"Please do not treat me like an idiot Alex. Of course, I came here to see you, is that what you want to hear? I read your stupid letters, and I was willing to give you the benefit of the doubt, but today I realised how naive I was to make the same mistake twice."

The look of hurt turned to one of confusion.

"What are you talking about? Why are you the one giving me the benefit of the doubt? You just stopped talking to me, Kacy! I didn't know why or what I did wrong, but somehow I am to blame?"

I had seen it with my own two eyes that very afternoon. Her fabrications would not be accepted anymore.

"I stopped talking to you? Alex, why will you not just admit that you were cheating on me with Jennifer? It was obvious. You didn't text me back for days, and she answered your phone for god's sake, Alex, stop lying to me!!!"

The anger raged through my body. How dare she take me for a fool. My outburst caused an old couple at the bar to look our way. The ability to stand was no longer second nature; my legs felt feeble, shaky. The seat across from where Alex had been sat appealed greatly.

"I never cheated on you, Kacy; I would never do that. I loved you too much. I would have never hurt you like that. You have to believe me."

How could I believe anything she said? Then something clicked. Her facial expression changed to one of considerable unease.

"Wait, what do you mean Jennifer answered my phone?"

"What I said, Alex. You said in your letter that you *'lost your phone'* if that were true, why did Jennifer answer it the next day?"

The creases in her forehead grew deeper as she contemplated what that meant.

"I am so confused Kacy. If Jennifer answered my phone, what did she say?"

If? Did she think I was lying? I reigned in my frustration and responded as the polite old couple would have liked. Less screaming.

"She said you had left your phone at her house the night before and that she would let you know I had called. The conversation was barely 60 seconds long."

As if breaking news to Alex, she put her head in her hands.

"I swear to you, Kacy, I lost my phone. Jennifer did not find it until days later. I went to her house that night because she was having a housewarming party, and…Rose told me I should get out of the house. When I finally got my phone back, I had no contact from you. Your phone went straight to voicemail when I tried to call, I even text Whitney, and she told me to leave you alone. I had no idea what I'd done wrong, Kacy."

The way she choked up when she said Rose's name sent a shiver down my spine, I did not want to ask just then, but I feared the worst had already happened.

"If that is the truth, Alex, then how do you explain what I just saw earlier today? You and Jennifer are together, are you not?"

Her gaze dropped from mine and towards the floor; I was right.

"It started a few weeks ago. I swear to you I never had any interest in Jennifer when I was with you, Kacy."

"Oh, and all of a sudden you do now? Do you think I'm stupid?"

She pleaded her innocence.

"Kacy, you didn't reply to any of my letters. You didn't text me or call me. I was heartbroken."

I sniggered sarcastically.

"Obviously not that heartbroken, considering you moved on

immediately!!"

The last part left my mouth from a place of pure anger. If I did not get angry, I would get upset, which was not what I wanted.

"It wasn't like that. I decided two weeks ago that it was time to move on, and well, Jennifer was just there. Things just happened, I can't explain it, but not one day has gone by that I haven't thought about you, Kace."

Despite the sincerity in her voice, I struggled to believe her every word.

"You should have tried harder, Alex. Why did you not try harder?"

I spoke just above a whisper, knowing that the words weren't solely aimed at Alex.

"I know, and I regret that now. I wanted to fly out to Raleigh, I did. I looked for a flight on more than one occasion, but in all honestly, my pride took over. I was too embarrassed at how you just dropped me. I didn't want to show you how hurt I was because I genuinely thought that you had found somebody else."

She sighed.

"How did we let our wires get so crossed?"

I asked. Our feelings of pride had prevailed.

"I don't know. I should have known that none of it made sense. I was so quick to assume the worst, and for that, I am truly sorry."

Alex reached across the table for my hand; I pulled away, unable to allow such intimacy.

"There was another reason I was so intent on cutting you from my life. A text message. If you did lose your phone, I can only assume she replied to the message I sent and not you."

The bewilderment was genuine.

"What message? What did she say?"

"I tried calling you several times the day after the party; eventually, Jennifer answered. She said you would be collecting your phone from her that night, and when I didn't hear anything from you at all the next day, I sent a message demanding answers. I wanted to know what I had done to deserve such treatment from you. The reply I got simply said *'I am sorry'* with no explanation, no justification, so that is when I decided to cut you from my life because I assumed that is what you wanted."

Alex rubbed her forehead, the strain becoming recognisable.

"Oh…so that's why you didn't speak to me? That is why Whitney would not speak to me either. You assumed I had just abandoned you for Jennifer. As if I would ever do that. I am so sorry for everything, Kacy. You must believe me when I say I would never intentionally hurt you. Jennifer is nothing compared to you; she has been a mere distraction over the past few weeks, nothing more."

It was becoming clear that only one person was responsible for the pain I had suffered, and that was not Alex.

"I believe you."

I hoped saying the words aloud would make them all together true. It made sense. Alex stood from her seated position across from me and walked around the table to kneel beside me.

"I can't believe I have had to endure missing you uncontrollably for the past five weeks because of her. Torturing myself every night, thinking you are lying in someone else's arms because I was not good enough for you."

Alex had experienced the heartache all the same.

"I just can't get my head around why she would act that way? I find it so hard to believe. She is either a very nasty person or very unstable."

I was not sure which I would prefer. Alex pondered.

"I thought she was a bit too full-on from the start. When I told her I had a girlfriend, she didn't like it; I could just tell. I didn't mention anything to you because I wanted to give her the benefit of the doubt; no way did I think she would pull something like this. I should have known something was off, how she just randomly found my phone days after and come to think of it, she was so eager to message you on social media on my behalf, she played the good friend card, she didn't want you worrying were her exact words. How could I have been so stupid?"

Her eyes glazed over. Her heartbreak was mirroring my own. I was utterly lost for words, the rollercoaster of emotions coming out victorious.

"You are not stupid. You just always want to see the best in people; that's not a fault."

Alex lifted her arm to brush the hair behind my ear, how I had missed her touch.

"I have missed you so much."

The words she spoke were barely above a whisper. I broke down in the main lobby, unable to control the emotion anymore. The guests strolled by, getting an eyeful of the scene as it unfolded, but my concern was not with them. The tears poured without warning; Alex moved in closer to my side to console me. I felt her arm close around my waist as the other came up to wipe away the tears. Pulling away proved difficult; my resolve had been broken. All I could think about was her touch. The way she smelt so perfectly and fit so comfortably beside me was enslaving. Naively or not, I believed her side of the story. The person Alex was, did not coincide with the heartless figure I had created. She was kind, caring, sweet, protective, and loving.

Why had I been so quick to deny that?

The whole time her heart had been breaking uncontrollably, just like mine. I looked into her eyes, and my world felt whole again. Despite the turmoil and the heartbreak, one thing had never wavered from the moment I laid eyes on her. I loved her. I would always love her.

The happiness I had not felt since the moment she left surrounded me as her arms took me entirely in her embrace. We sat that way for a while; no more conversation was needed, just the ability to be comforted by her was enough. As soon as my tears started to dry, a sudden realisation hit Alex; she darted upright and took off for the door.

"Alex, where are you going?"

"I am going to see Jennifer; I want an explanation for why she ruined my life. How could she do that? I need to find out."

"Wait...are you going to come back?"

It was more of a request than a question.

"Of course I will. We need to catch up on so much, but I need to deal with this first. I will be back later, I promise."

She paused and stepped back towards me.

"Did you want to say something?"

Only the obvious.

"I love you, Alex. I never stopped. I just need you to know that."

She took my hand in hers and kissed it gently, followed by my forehead and then finally my lips. The kiss was brief, but the taste of her lingered on my lips. Leaving me wanting so much more.

"I love you too, Kacy, more than you will ever know."

I watched her walk away, with only the hope that she would return soon. The show in the lobby had gone on long enough. I gathered myself and made my way back to room 34. Before I had the chance to shut the door behind me, Whitney pounced.

"KACY!! I have been waiting up here, pacing around,

twiddling my thumbs, biting my nails. What has happened? You were gone for ages!!"

She went quiet when she spied my puffy eyes and mascara-streaked face.

"Kace, are you okay?"

"I think I am better than okay. I think everything is going to be just fine."

I explained to Whitney word for word what Alex had said. She believed her just like I did. She always trusted my judgement, so if I believed her, so would she. We spoke for the next hour about expectations now that the truth had come to light, but that was still unknown. Only time would tell was my best answer.

Whitney's disliking of Jennifer was brutally hilarious. It was called for considering the woman had ruined my relationship and stolen my girlfriend. I wanted to meet her; I wanted to see if she had any remorse for what she had done. Clearly, deception was something she was good at. Maybe she had a long history of it; I could only hope that Alex would see through the lies, second time lucky. I had a feeling it would not be the last time Jennifer became a thorn in my side.

I was on the verge of sleep when the Hotel phone rang, the clock showed 10:32 pm, it had been a long day, my eyes were sore from the obscene amount of crying, and Alex was yet to return. Sleep seemed like my best option.

"Hello."

"Hello Miss Sullivan, you have a call waiting at reception. Would you like me to transfer it through to your room?"

"Yes, that would be great, thanks."

"No problem Miss Sullivan. Have a good evening."

The receiver clicked, and a new voice appeared on the other end of the line.

"Hi, is that Kacy?"

I expected to hear Alex's voice; instead, it was a woman's voice that sounded vaguely familiar.

"Yes, it is. Can I ask who's speaking?"

I think I already knew what the response would be. There was silence before the unknown caller introduced themself.

"It's Jennifer. I am sure you know me by now?"

She had some nerve.

"I don't know you, no. What I know of you, though, is unflattering, to say the least."

How dare she call me.

"That is interesting. I will get straight to the point."

This ought to be good, I thought.

"You need to leave town and stop this ridiculous crusade of trying to win Alex back. You had your chance with her, and now she has moved on with someone else. Whatever little plan you have got in that head of yours will fail. I will make sure of it."

I placed the receiver on loudspeaker, so Whitney had the pleasure of hearing the conversation unfold.

"I am sorry. Are you threatening me?"

"Not at all, just a mere warning. You see, there is a significant difference between you and me."

"Oh really? What is that then?"

Enlighten me. She was quick to respond.

"I would not have let the love of my life go as easily as you did. You really didn't put up a fight at all, did you? I was quite disappointed. I expected a bit more from you."

Did she think this was a game?

"You don't even know me. You have some nerve to call me after what you did."

Jennifer's laugh sounded unnerving.

"What I did was get the girl I wanted, and now you are causing me some problems. Whatever you told Alex has upset her. I don't like it when she's upset. She has blamed me for your breakup and taken every little word that's come from your mouth and believed it. I will give you credit for that, but once she gets to my house, I will be able to smooth things over, don't you worry about that."

Did she believe her own lies?

"So, you don't think you are to blame? At all? I told Alex nothing but the truth."

Jennifer mocked me. She was older than me but seemed so immature.

"The truth is whatever you want it to be, Kacy Sullivan. She will forgive me in time because she loves me more than she ever loved you. I was there for her when she needed someone; when Rose passed, I was there, not you."

Whitney's eyes were ablaze with fury. I could tell she wanted so desperately to give Jennifer a piece of her mind, but I had to deal with it myself. My fear that Rose had passed was confirmed.

"You were there for her because your lies meant that I couldn't be. Let's not get things twisted, Jennifer. The only reason Alex has given you the time of day is because she thought she couldn't have me. You know that as well as I do."

Jennifer laughed again, this time, uncontrollably. She was trying everything she could to aggravate me. I would not let her win.

"Just do us all a favour, Kacy and leave town. Don't make this harder than it needs to be."

What would she do exactly? Fight me? Try to run me off the road? I refused to let her think she scared me. With Whitney by my side, she would have to come at us with the full force of everything she had, that I knew for sure. The words that followed came from a place of pure hatred, one that rarely ever surfaced.

"Listen, Jennifer, I know the type of person you are. Alex is only with you because she thought she had lost me. You are not the first choice, nor will you ever be. If I leave tomorrow, do you think Alex will not follow? What else is keeping her here? God bless Rose, she was the only reason Alex moved to this town. You know her life is in Raleigh, so I'm afraid you have no supporting arguments. I don't know what you think you are achieving by calling me; if you think I am scared of you and your threats, then you are sincerely mistaken."

I took a deep breath before finishing.

"I would like to know just one thing before we end this delightful phone call. Have you always struggled to get your own girlfriends? And lastly, have you always been this crazy? Because I think you would benefit from seeing a professional."

Whitney burst out laughing. The line went dead.

"Kace, honestly, you could not have handled that any better. Our dear friend Jennifer clearly didn't have a reply to that, did she?"

I placed the phone back in its cradle and automatically high fived Whitney.

"Wait, what if she turns out to be a serial killer? Or even just a regular woman that is willing to murder for love? I mean, neither bodes well for us, does it."

She had a point; I didn't know what I was dealing with. The quicker I got out of Cannon Beach, the better.

"I mean, the girl is crazy, but let's hope that's not the case. Do you remember Sarah Brooks from high school? Jennifer reminds me a lot of her. She went completely off the rails after the first year of college, apparently tried to kill her husband with a screwdriver!"

Whitney's eyes widened.

"Yes, I do remember her! They do have remarkably similar attributes. Anyway, what are you going to do now? Maybe you should call Alex?"

That would prove difficult with no contact details.

"I don't have her phone number. I just assumed she would come back here after she had been to see Jennifer. It's late now though, isn't it? I'm sure she will come through in the morning."

I could only hope with so much still unresolved. My mind returned to Rose; she must have passed recently. The thought was utterly heartbreaking. A pang of guilt entered my body because I had not been there for her to hold her hand through one of the hardest moments of her life. As heartbreaking as the loss of her grandmother was, it meant there was nothing else keeping her in Oregon. Alex's apartment, her bar and all her friends were in Raleigh. I could only assume she was still in Oregon to tie up any loose ends or was Jennifer keeping her there? I needed answers to my questions, and I needed them fast. The clock showed it was roughly 18 hours until we were due to depart back to Raleigh.

CHAPTER FIFTEEN

The alarm on my phone sounded; it was 8 am. I awoke several times in the night to check my phone, hoping I would see a text from Alex, but I soon realised that was not possible; she didn't have my new number. Disappointment set in. My morning routine was well underway when Whitney woke an hour later. Breakfast in the hotel was served between 7 and 10 am; another guest told me that it was not to be missed. It took Whitney a mere 15 minutes to get ready; she really was a natural beauty, no make-up needed to make her look as impressive as she did. By 9 am, I was sat around the breakfast table in the far corner of the dining room. The view of Cannon Beach could be seen perfectly through a break in the trees.

We very quickly settled with our food, cereal for me and fruit with yoghurt for Whitney. The conversation started to flow.

"Do you think Alex will come this morning?"

Whitney barely managed to get out the words, contending with a mouthful of fruit.

"I hope so. She promised me she would be back later. I didn't even get the chance to tell her I was only here until this afternoon."

My spoon dipped in and out of the cereal repetitively; my

appetite had been lacklustre since we arrived.

"Well, we need to go and find her, don't we? We can pack our stuff and leave them at reception."

I rummaged around in my brown satchel bag to find my diary. I looked at her address once again; it was still there.

"I should have asked Alex if she was still there. What if she's moved?"

That concerned me.

"Don't look so worried; it will all work out just fine. I have a good feeling about this. The two of you just need some time alone to talk things through, or at least trade phone numbers; we aren't living in the dark ages, Kace."

I laughed and almost choked on a piece of cereal.

"You are totally right; exchanging phone numbers is necessary. I don't know why, but I am kind of nervous."

"Nervous about what?"

Everything, I thought.

"Just being around her again, it's scary, the thought of opening myself back up to her."

"You told me last night how easy it felt to be with her again. You said it felt like no time at all had passed. That is exactly what it will be like. You still love her, right?"

That was the one thing I was certain about.

"I will always love her, Whit; I can't explain it. Even though we have been apart for all this time, it feels like she is still mine. I never stopped loving her even when I thought the worst of her; that is why I know she is the one for me. It's like nothing I have ever felt before."

I smiled at the thought of Alex, of being with her again; nothing made me happier.

"Look at you with that grin on your face. It's so nice to see a genuine smile again. You deserve to be happy, Kace."

"I hope we can be Whit; I really do."

There was a pleasant silence whilst we both finished our breakfast. The hotel kitchen staff started to clear away the hot breakfast, followed by the cereals, and it was time to go. It took no longer than 10 minutes to pack our belongings and do one last sweep of the room. We checked our bags in at reception, and they offered to order us a taxi, which arrived on the dot. My nerves started to get the better of me during the cab ride. Whitney squeezed my hand every few minutes, offering her support as best she could. I was going out on a whim arriving at an address I was not sure she lived at anymore. I had no way of contacting her other than the scribbled first line of her address and area code that my diary contained.

We pulled up promptly. The beach house was not what I expected, but it was somewhere I could imagine living myself. The exterior was beautifully painted a dark red, with a fresh white porch and a white door. The number 42 in big silver numerals stood out; I had arrived.

There was only a tiny garden to the front, with a driveway and garage to the left. I knew the primary features would be to the rear of the property; with it being a beach house, the views were bound to be immense. The property looked very well maintained, like most properties on the street, a fresh new hanging basket lay to the right of the door, with several plant pots to the left, leading up and onto the porch a small chair sat still in the windless air. It was picturesque, the perfect postcard for what seemed like the ideal little coastal town.

On further inspection, there were no cars parked in the driveway, no windows open or doors ajar, no sign of any life inside the house.

"Go on, go and knock. I will wait here."

Whitney nudged me towards the steps, slamming me back into reality. Three consecutive raps on the door were all it took to realise that nobody was coming to open it. The piercing doorbell was loud enough to alert anyone within the vicinity that a visitor was waiting at the door.

"Maybe she's in the shower? Or down at the beach?"

Whitney called from the pavement; she was clutching at anything she could for my sake.

"Let's go and take a look." She said.

The back of the house was as I expected. The view of the beach, sea and surrounding coastal towns made it the perfect holiday home. In that moment, I could see why Rose wanted to go there; it was a place she held dear to her heart. Often, she had spent her summers there with her husband and her children and eventually her grandchildren. It was a walk down memory lane for Rose, a time to remember everything her life had been and had become. What better way to leave this life than in a place where you truly lived it, a place where you could be at peace with the world, knowing that on the other side, you would be reunited with the people that made that place so special. I saw the appeal instantly. I hoped one day, I too would have a place like Cannon Beach.

Whitney overtook me and made her way down to the sloped pathway to see if she could spot Alex.

"Anything down there, Whit?" I yelled.

I had peered through every window and tried the locks on both doors. The neighbours would be on high alert, no doubt, I half expected a patrol car to arrive. The inside looked so inviting and warm, and the brick walls had been accompanied by a beautiful, soft, leather, brown sofa. Stacks of wood displayed neatly at the side of the fire made for a cosy atmosphere. The interior was unusual for a beach house. It was like taking the inside of a cabin from Alaska's cold depths and placing it in the sunny beachside resort. Unusual yet beautiful.

"Nothing Kace, any luck up there?"

"No, there is no sign of anyone inside. The house looks so

neat and tidy through the windows. Maybe she isn't staying here anymore."

My attempt at hiding the disappointment failed.

"Maybe we should have a closer look. Surely there is a key somewhere around here…"

Whitney rummaged underneath each plant pot, one after the other.

"…everyone leaves a spare key outside in small towns like this, or is that just in the movies."

The police would soon be alerted if they weren't already.

"I don't think we can just enter someone's house without permission Whit. People get in trouble for that."

She continued to rummage but produced nothing.

"Well, it's clear we are not in the movies; it would certainly be easier than this."

She let out a loud sigh in perfect harmony with my own.

"Now what?"

The only words I could manifest, chosen from an overwhelming swarm of thoughts that clouded my head.

"Do you think it's a sign? Someone is telling me I shouldn't be trying to dredge up the past anymore."

"Don't be ridiculous. Nothing makes more sense than you being here."

I could not be so sure anymore. Why hadn't she returned to the B&B? What could be taking her so long?

"Why didn't I ask her for her number before she left? Then there would be none of this hassle. I was just so certain she would come back last night. Do you think I was hoping for too much by coming here?"

I sat down on the porch steps, sapped of the brief joy I had experienced the night before.

"I think you need to stop blaming yourself, you followed your heart, and you did what you felt you needed to do. There are people out there that would not have taken a chance like you have, and those people will live to regret it for the rest of their lives, but you will be able to tell yourself that you didn't give up. No matter what happens."

Whitney was right; she always was.

"Now you just need to leave it up to Alex; the ball is in her court. I'm sure when she's dealt with whatever she needs to she will come back to you."

I smiled my best smile at my absolute best friend. She was the one person in my life that I knew would always know what to say when words were beyond me.

"Why don't you leave her a note? Then when she comes back, she has a way of contacting you? And if she doesn't live here anymore, then the person who does next will be extremely confused."

We laughed at the possibility. Well, there was no harm in trying, I concluded.

"That's a clever idea."

I searched around, amongst a book, some sweets, and my headphones was my trusty diary with several blank pages at the back. I preceded to jot down what I was feeling inside.

Alex,
I don't know what happened last night. You didn't come back, so I came to your house, at least I think this is still your house. You weren't here, obviously. So, I had no other choice but to leave and head back to Raleigh. I just want you to know that I looked for you; I didn't just go. I have missed you so much over the past few months; you have no idea.
Last night just brought back a flood of memories, it made me realise just how in love with you I still am, and I think always will be. I am so sorry things turned out the way they did. I am sorry I didn't believe you, the first thing I seem to do is doubt

people. I should have known better with you.
I fly out at 5:30 today. If you read this note before then, I would love to see you. I need to see you. I love you, Alex. I hope you still feel the same too.
Goodbye for now.
Kacy

P.S. My new number is written on the back of this letter. I hope to hear from you soon.

I carefully tore out the piece of paper, folding it three ways before I posted it through the antique-looking black letterbox. My last hope and my last resort wrote upon a scrap of paper. I hoped it would find its way to Alex, knowing that I was all out of options if it did not.

"There, it's done. I need a drink."

"Little early for an alcoholic beverage I think Kace, maybe a coffee?"

Come to think of it; I don't think I could have stomached an alcoholic drink.

I left the beach house, shadowed by a cloud of uncertainty. The notion that everything would work out for the best firmly cemented in my subconscious.

What that meant was undetermined. The next five hours would reveal all.

CHAPTER SIXTEEN

Alex

"Jennifer, you need to leave me alone now. I have heard everything you have had to say, and you are just repeating yourself. I don't want to hear it so please, just leave."

I fiddled in my pocket for my house keys. Why were they always out of reach at the most inappropriate times? I needed to get away from the constant screeching coming from Jennifer. I knew what she was trying to do. Kacy had opened my eyes to the truth that was now so clear. She would do anything she could to try and worm her way back in, but I was prepared for that and loaded with the truth as my ally.

"No, Alex. I am not leaving until you admit that you love me and that your feelings for me are real."

The woman was unbelievable and relentless. What a combination.

"Love? Jennifer, we have been dating for two weeks and the whole time, it has been one big lie. How could I possibly love you?"

I finally found my keys and began to open the front door. My only thought being how do I make it even more abundantly clear that I wanted nothing to do with her anymore. It was proving extremely difficult.

"Don't make out like what I did was an awful thing. I did it because I wanted you. I knew there was something between us ever since the first day you came to town."

I sarcastically sneered.

"You think that sabotaging my relationship wasn't an awful thing to do? You are more deluded than I thought."

I entered the front door; uninvited, Jennifer pushed her way through behind me. My home for the past three months was one I had become incredibly fond of and one that Jennifer had made herself all too comfortable in over the past two weeks.

"I didn't sabotage it. Stop saying that. I merely gave it a push in the direction it was going to go down eventually. Do you not feel what I have felt ever since you came here? Something brought you back into my life, you came back here for a reason and I think that reason was to meet me."

I was trapped in a conversation I had already endured the night before; the repetition was draining. I had been to Jennifer's house, spent the whole night arguing over the obvious and now I just wanted to shower, change, and go and see Kacy. That was the only thing keeping me sane.

"The reason I ended up here was because my grandma was dying. I find it hard to see your point of view if I am completely honest."

She rolled her eyes as if I were the one being ridiculous.

"Look, Jennifer, you had no right to interfere with my personal life. You saw how heartbroken I was after me and Kacy split up, and you just stood there knowing full well that you were the cause. How could you even do that? I don't know you anymore. I thought you were a sweet girl, so kind and innocent. Clearly, I was wrong."

I perched on the edge of the brown leather sofa I had grown to love. Jennifer situated herself beside me, unwelcome.

"Alex, just admit that you love me. We can make this work;

I know we can. I did it all for us, can't you see that? All I want is to make you happy."

What did I need to do to get it through to her? 10 hours of conversation had done nothing to change her perspective.

"I do not love you, Jennifer. I have never loved you. Yes, I admit I liked you, but that was not real. You made me feel that way because you poisoned my head with thoughts of Kacy cheating on me and not wanting me anymore. You made me feel like I needed you when it was all a lie. So, I am sorry, but it doesn't matter how many times you repeat yourself. It will not change the truth. I don't love you."

The words felt harsh as they escaped my lips but given the circumstances, they needed to be said. I rose quickly and went to the fridge to pour myself a drink. I half expected Jennifer to latch onto my body as she had previously done four times through the night.

The desire to leave had been apparent, but Jennifer had proceeded to make it difficult. I did not expect Kacy to understand, I wanted nothing more than to return to The Lighthouse Inn to spend time with her, but I had to deal with the loose ends to ensure there would be no more drama in our future.

It seemed unkind to think of Jennifer as a *loose end* as if she could be so easily brushed to the side, but my patience had worn thin. That morning just when I assumed I had escaped Jennifer, I caught a glimpse of her car in my rear-view mirror on the journey home. She was not giving up without a fight.

Jennifer was uncharacteristically quiet as I made my way back into the living room. I caught her reading a small piece of paper.

"What are you reading?"

Jennifer instantly looked alarmed.

"Nothing, just something I had in my pocket."

She was lying.

"Jennifer, don't you think you have lied to me enough?"

There had been a piece of paper on the floor in amongst the post when I entered. I had glanced towards it but hadn't felt the need to pick it up. I walked back towards the door to discover that the same piece of paper was no longer there.

"I know you picked it up from my post. Hand it over."

The guilty look on her face was now one that seemed so familiar. How had I not noticed the signs earlier?

"What is it with her, Alex? Why is she so much better than me? Your perfect little Kacy can't do a thing wrong, can she?"

The bitterness filled the atmosphere between us. Was the piece of paper from Kacy? I had to know what it said.

"Kacy is the love of my life. She has been since the moment I laid eyes on her. Why can you not grasp that? I'm sorry, but I am not the person for you. You might think I am right now, but you will find someone else who loves you for you. You can't honestly believe that a relationship can last when it starts dishonestly."

My voice broke slightly, strained from the hours of conversing and getting no further. It was finally taking its toll.

"The love of your life? You have known me longer than her. How can you even say someone is the love of your life when you have known them for less than a year. It's ridiculous."

The time scale did not matter to me. It was merely a social construct.

"You have known me for three months Jennifer, and you claim you are madly in love with me, so clearly there is a slight contradiction somewhere, isn't there. Anyway, I don't have time for this anymore. I don't want to argue with you. I don't want to hear any more excuses. I just want you to give me that piece of paper and leave. Please."

Jennifer looked down at the piece of paper in her hands then back at me. She smiled before she ripped the letter into tiny pieces, throwing them onto the hardwood floor at my feet.

"Here, there's your stupid piece of paper. When you realise that you got it wrong, you know where you can find me."

Jennifer advanced to the door at speed.

"Don't hold your breath, Jennifer. Thank you for making this such an easy decision."

I shouted after her as she stormed down the steps and sped away in her beaten up Volvo. The relief was all I felt. I shut the door behind her and immediately went to try and piece the paper back together. It was Kacy's writing; all I could seem to string together were two sentences.

"I don't know what happened…You weren't here, obviously. So, I had no other choice…realise just how in love with…I am sorry I didn't believe you…P.S. my number is printed…"

Where was her number printed? I searched frantically through the bits of paper but could not see any numbers. No matter which way I put the pieces back together, it didn't add up, it was as if a piece or even two were missing. I double-checked the floor in the living room several times, rearranging the furniture to check it had not slid underneath; there was no sign of any remaining pieces. I slumped down on the kitchen stool, totally and utterly defeated.

It was just after 2 pm; I had to see Kacy. I called the B&B and the clerk insisted the two young girls staying in room 34 had, in fact, checked out that morning. I knew I had to leave right away if I had any chance of catching Kacy at the airport. The airport was 30 minutes away, maybe even 45 with traffic. I had no idea of her flight time, for all I knew, she could have already left, and that filled me with fear.

What now? That was the ultimate question. What did I have

in Oregon now? Rose was gone; she was not coming back. That broke my heart every single day. Natalie had already flown back to Raleigh a few days after the funeral to restart her life there. She insisted on retaking charge of the bar and trying her best to get back to normal. I missed Natalie, I missed my friends, and most importantly, I missed Kacy. Raleigh was my life; it always had been.

There was a knock at the door. I grabbed my keys, ready to leave. Please don't be Jennifer, I begged. I closed my eyes; hand placed firmly on the door handle. I inhaled deeply, preparing myself for the worst. On a count of three, I opened the door to find an unexpected familiar face.

"Charlotte?"

The short, blonde-haired woman who stood before me was Jennifer's sister, Charlotte Locksley.

"Hi Alex, do you have a minute?"

I hadn't seen Charlotte since the funeral two weeks prior.

"I am in a bit of a rush actually, can it wait?"

Please say yes.

"Not really. It's something I think you should know."

Charlotte looked concerned. I was too polite to say no; there was no other option.

"Okay, come in."

I walked through to the kitchen and placed my keys back on the counter. Although terrible timing, I hated to be ill-mannered; hospitality was ingrained into my soul.

"Can I get you a drink?"

She shook her head.

"No, I just had a coffee on the way over, but thank you."

Charlotte pointed towards the bar stool.

"Of course, please. Take a seat."

My mind was screaming, *why are you here*, but my body kept the same composure it was accustomed to.

"I am sorry to barge in on you like this, Alex. Jennifer isn't due to come over, is she?"

I perked up as soon as she mentioned Jennifer. Why did she look so alarmed at the prospect?

"No, she won't be."

"I just thought I would check. I know she should be at the café today, but I didn't want her to find me here and it cause a lot of hassle. "

I was intrigued. Why exactly would that cause so much hassle?

"What is it you want to tell me, Charlotte? I assume it's about Jennifer?"

She fiddled with the ends of her hair, clearly nervous.

"If I tell you this Alex, you can't tell Jennifer I am the reason you found out. She can't know I was ever here. She would never forgive me. Promise?"

"Okay, I promise."

Curiosity killed the cat.

"I am telling you because I like you. You are a good person and I think you deserve to know the truth."

The build-up to whatever she wanted to reveal was uneasy. I nodded in acknowledgement of the sacrifice she was making. This was hard for Charlotte to do, I could see that in the way she anxiously played with the buckle on her bag. The way she blinked out of sync, uncharacteristically. I waited patiently for the words to come.

"I was alarmed at the funeral when I saw how close the two of you were; she was in sync with you the whole day. There's a look she gets when she wants something and nothing or nobody will stop her from getting it. She's been the same ever since we were kids. She has had that look for a while now. I was surprised to see that your girlfriend wasn't there to support you. I asked your sister at the wake; she said you had recently split. I didn't want to pry. I know the timing wasn't appropriate, so I left it at that."

I took a seat on the stool opposite Charlotte. I feared it was not going to be a quick conversation.

"When I bumped into Natalie at the café a few days later, I asked her why things had ended with you and Kacy. She gave me the watered-down version of events I would imagine, but something didn't sit right with me. It felt all too familiar. I felt obliged to tell you, to warn you, but I struggled to find the courage until now. She is my sister, after all, but that doesn't mean I agree with the things she does."

Charlotte knew what Jennifer was capable of, but how? I sat in silence, urging her to continue.

"About two months before you came to town, a young woman called Olivia lived here. Her parents divorced when she was 17. She chose to live with her dad in San Francisco for the first five years and then she moved here to stay with her mom, about ten months ago now. When she came to town, like anyone new, it was the same with you; she was the talk of Cannon Beach for a while. Fresh meat, I guess you could say. The men fancied her; the women wanted to be her. She started coming into the café daily for her morning coffee. I noticed as the weeks went by that Jennifer had grown fond of Olivia. She would make sure she always worked the early shift; even on her days off, she would call in *'just to check everything was alright'* conveniently at the same time Olivia would be there."

The name Olivia rang a bell. Some of Jennifer's friends had mentioned her, never in much detail, sworn to secrecy almost.

"So, after a month, Jennifer started going for food with her, for drinks, to the beach. It turned out Olivia was also gay. Olivia had a long-term girlfriend back in San Francisco. She would talk about her often and the excitement of her coming to visit. That bothered Jennifer, the more time they spent together, the more I could see it affected her. She was jealous; I could see straight through her. Fast forward another month; Olivia came running into the café crying, looking for Jennifer to console her. Apparently, her girlfriend had broken up with her. Just like that, she ignored her phone calls, ignored her messages. The poor girl was distraught."

The story sounded all too well known.

"Jennifer played the perfect friend card. She was there as her shoulder to cry on. One thing led to another and their relationship became more intimate. This continued for over a month. That is until the real reason why Olivia's girlfriend had split up with her was revealed. Olivia had gone back to San Francisco to attend one of her best friends birthday parties. Her ex-girlfriend turned up, and things became heated. Her ex revealed text messages and photos that had been sent to her from Jennifer claiming they'd been having an affair since she moved to Cannon Beach."

My eyes enlarged, shocked at how recognisable the story appeared. It seemed Jennifer had a history of repeating herself.

"Olivia returned to Cannon Beach, came storming into the cafe furiously shouting at Jennifer, claiming she was out of control, crazy, insane, you name it. The text messages sent to Olivia's ex were all conjured up by Jennifer. She had two phones and sent messages between the two to make it look like they were having this illicit affair. The photos were already on Olivia's phone; she had plans to send them to her girlfriend as a surprise. Jennifer must have had access to her phone one day; that wouldn't have been too difficult for her. When confronted, Jennifer denied it all, but the evidence was there. I know when Jenny is lying, better than anyone and it was written all over her face that she was responsible."

It all seemed so surreal. Why had nobody warned me earlier? Were they frightened of Jennifer?

"So what did Olivia do?"

"She left town. Moved back to San Francisco about a week later. Jennifer proclaimed her innocence to everyone that knew her, but many believed Olivia's version of events. She still denies it to this day. With a lot of people, it gave Jennifer a bit of a reputation. Once you guys got so close, the whispers started. I didn't want to believe that she would do something like that again. That's why I didn't speak to you sooner. I confronted Jennifer about it last week and she told me to stay out of her business. I'm not saying she has had something to do with your break-up, but I think you should consider it. Dig a little deeper. That's my advice to you, Alex."

Charlotte was unaware that her story was too late. The damage had already been done.

"I know about Jennifer sabotaging my relationship. I found out and confronted her yesterday. She is very creative when she wants to be. Believe it or not, she didn't deny it. She made out as though she had been doing me a favour. She believes her own lies and that's the scary part."

Charlotte lowered her head, ashamed.

"I am so sorry, Alex. I have thought about asking her to see someone, a therapist maybe. There must be a reason why she does these things. She was the perfect child growing up; she couldn't do a thing wrong in my parent's eyes; she still can't. They would believe her over me any day of the week and that's so frustrating. I feel like I can't tell them."

How many more times would Jennifer deceive and lie to get what she wanted? How much further was she willing to go? Would someone get hurt next time?

"I understand you are in a tricky situation Charlotte. Don't worry about me. I found out the truth now and not years down the line; that's a relief. I have the chance to fix what Jennifer did; the next person might not. Why can't she just go for someone available? Is it the chase? Is she that sadistic that she enjoys ruining people's lives?"

I didn't expect Charlotte to have all the answers. There was a flash of irritation, a defence mechanism.

"I don't think she's sadistic. She is still my sister, and it's hard for me to see her make these choices because I can't defend what she's done. You knew her when we were growing up; she was kind and thoughtful, very much the ideal child. I know that doesn't excuse what she's done, but I was hoping by telling you that you might find it in your heart to forgive her? To at least try and talk some sense into her? She speaks so highly of you, Alex. I feel like she would listen."

After everything Jennifer had done, forgiving her felt improbable. Charlotte had some nerve.

"So you want me to help her? After everything she's done? Come on, Charlotte, you can't expect that of me."

Oh, but she did. Her intentions had seemed somewhat genuine when she arrived. Turning up on a whim to help me see the truth, to allow me to break free from the spell I was under, except her ulterior motive was one that would benefit her sister and ultimately her. She didn't want to confront Jennifer herself, but she also didn't want the shame of another *'incident'*. I imagine people looked at Charlotte differently, whispered behind her back about how her sister was unconventional, shall we say. I could only imagine how hard it was for her.

"I know it's a lot to ask. I know what she's done is terrible, and I would never condone that. I just don't know what else to do. Most people would just turn their back on her, but surely there is a part of you that cares for her. Maybe enough to try and see past what she's done?"

My forehead wrinkled under pressure, confused. What she was asking was absurd.

"I don't belong here, Charlotte; this isn't my life. Jennifer isn't my responsibility. I did care for her, but whatever I felt for her has been seriously compromised over the past 24 hours. She feels no remorse for what she's done. I can't help someone like that."

It was the truth. The night before, I had despised Jennifer for what she had done, but that quickly turned to pity.

"I understand. I don't know what your plans are, Alex, but I have enjoyed you being here. A lot of people are incredibly fond of you."

"I appreciate that. I don't mean to be rude, but I really do need to head out unless there's anything else?"

Time was of the essence.

"Are you leaving town?"

"I will be eventually. Like I said, I don't belong here."

Charlotte looked sad at the prospect.

"I disagree. You have always belonged here. That's why you settled in so easily when you came back."

The sentiment was sweet. Cannon Beach had always felt so comfortable to me. I reached for my keys. My eagerness to leave visible.

"Thank you, Charlotte. That's very kind of you to say."

"I know you don't owe me anything, but can I ask you a favour?"

She was taking advantage of my good nature, but I nodded and obliged.

"Will you go and see Jennifer at some point before you leave town? For what it's worth, I think she really does love you. She wouldn't have…"

Love was a game to Jennifer. Who's to say I was any different? Charlotte was going out on a limb for her sister, playing with fire, knowing full well she would get burnt.

"She wouldn't have what?"

Charlotte had said too much. What was she hiding? She contemplated her response for a brief moment.

"The bench by the beach? It was Jennifer that paid for it. The truck full of fresh flowers that arrived at the funeral, that was Jennifer. The donation to the cancer ward under Rose's name, also Jennifer. I am the only one that knows. She isn't all that bad, Alex, despite some of the choices she's made."

A bench had been made and inscribed with my grandparent's names, placed in the very spot where they used to sit and watch the sunset. There had been no explanation; nobody came forward to claim the wonderful gesture. We assumed it was an old friend who wanted to remain anonymous. The flowers, like nothing I had ever experienced, bouquet after bouquet lined the cemetery, a mix of white and red roses. I knew from experience how much funeral flowers cost and there had been no expense spared. Why would she do that? She hadn't done it so she could take credit, it was purely unselfish, or at least it seemed. Did she feel guilty for what she'd done?

"I didn't know any of that. I don't understand why she would do that? That is a lot of money to spend."

"Is it not obvious? She saw how much Rose meant to you, the sacrifices you made to come here. Jennifer loves you, Alex, whether you believe that or not. I think she felt she owed it to Rose for bringing you back to Cannon Beach."

It was all too obscuring. My mind told me to stay away from Jennifer, but my heart told me that there was a part of her worth saving. We all make mistakes.

"Did Jennifer put you up to this? You came in and told me the Olivia story it seemed to warn me, but now you want me to see the good in Jennifer, to give her another chance."

The narrative had flipped, which made me suspicious.

"She doesn't know I am here, I swear, but if you want to tell her, I will accept that. If it means you will go and see her and at least try to come to a resolve, then it won't have been in vain."

There was obviously a power struggle between Jennifer and Charlotte. Jennifer had always been the favourite. The popular one. The lucky one. Regardless of all that, she loved her sister. So much so that she was willing to accept the backlash it would cause by interfering. Deep down, I think Charlotte hoped that Jennifer would somehow turn a corner.

"I can't make any promises, Charlotte."

"Will you at least try?"

If I agreed, I didn't want my kindness to be misconstrued. I cared for Jennifer, my weakness being that I always saw the good in people, despite their many faults. The gestures brought to light changed things. Maybe Jennifer wasn't the callous, remorseless villain after all. Charlotte was pleading with my kind-hearted temperament. The decision should have been clear cut, but it wasn't. My moral compass was in turmoil. One informative conversation had brought about a newfound hesitation.

"I will try."

CHAPTER SEVENTEEN

It was almost 5 pm, we had been at the airport for two hours and the boarding would soon commence. We had spent the whole afternoon drinking coffee and browsing the boutiques in town, much to Whitney's delight. She was ecstatic when she finally bought the *'dress of her dreams'* as she called it. My mind had been completely pre-occupied throughout the whole experience.

Where was Alex?

What was she doing?

Did she get my letter?

The questions were nonstop. If only at that moment I could have flicked a switch, gone back to some form of normality were the discomfort wasn't at an all-time high. Life was not that simple.

"I guess she's not coming then."

I scanned the airport again, hoping and praying that Alex would appear.

"I don't think it's because she doesn't want to, Kace. Maybe she just hasn't seen the letter?"

The voice of reason.

"She loves you. You will figure it out."

Whitney had the faith that I did not.

"I hope that's enough. I love her too, more than anything. I just can't shake this feeling. I should be convinced that she would come back to me, but I'm not. We didn't have the chance to talk things through."

The reality of it, we had been apart for a long time; a brief conversation was all I had to go off.

"She told you she still loved you, Kace, that she'd missed you uncontrollably. If you want to know how she feels about you, that to me is as good as it gets. Hold onto that."

My phone vibrated once, a text message. The number on my screen had no contact assigned. Surely, it had to be Alex. I fumbled with the buttons, hurriedly trying to get to the message. Once I read the first line, I knew it was from Alex.

Kacy,
I thought about coming to the airport. I spent all night with Jennifer, and she told me the truth, her reasoning behind why she did it. It does not justify the lies, but it did make me realise that we have something more than I wanted to admit to myself. There is a lot you don't know about her, she isn't as vindictive as you think and I owe it to her to explore what we have.
I loved you once, Kacy, but so much has happened. If it helps you to move on, then please hate me; I deserve that. I wish you the best and I hope you find the right person for you. You will never hear from me again and I hope you can refrain from contacting me too. I think it would be best for us both.
Take care.
Alex

Breathing, a function our body subconsciously performs. It knows how much oxygen we need to not malfunction. I became consciously aware of my breathing in that moment, the rapid movement in my chest as it expanded. How could she do that to me? My mind raced. Jennifer must have poisoned her mind. What could she have said to get Alex to stay? She must have had something to hold against her. Would Alex have stayed if it were of her own free will?

One emotion prevailed above every other and that was my hate for Jennifer. I handed my phone to Whitney so she could see for herself.

"I can't believe her, Whit. After everything that Jennifer has done, she's choosing her?"

Whitney could only muster four words after the initial read-through of the message.

"I'm actually in shock."

That made two of us. It had to be a joke. Alex was about to run through the airport any minute and tell me it was all some cruel prank. Right? I was running purely on adrenaline, but the tank was almost empty. The reality would hit any minute.

"How can Jennifer ruin my relationship and get the girl? She is the bad person in all of this. Surely she can't win. That is not how this was supposed to end."

My eyes glazed over.

"I know, babe. I am so sorry. I did not expect it to go down like this. Alex's stupidity amazes me."

Pathetically my knees went weak at the thought of losing Alex forever. So many thoughts clouded my head, but I could not form a single sentence. It was different this time; I now had closure. I knew why she didn't want me and the reality was more excruciating than I ever could have imagined.

The airport intercom called out, momentarily removing me from the trance I found myself in.

"All passengers flying on the AR88446 flight to Raleigh, your gate is now ready for boarding."

A task as simple as standing seemed unachievable. I felt completely and utterly helpless. I had done all I could. I hoped that would comfort me someday.

"Come on, Kace, let's get out of here. It will all be okay; I promise you."

Whitney wrapped a tight arm around my waist and led me to the gate. How it would ever be okay again, I was not entirely sure. The trip to Cannon Beach had gone nothing like initially planned. It was ultimately the opposite.

"Thank you for being here for me, Whit. I would not have survived this weekend without you. I love you."

"Always. I love you too."

Have you ever felt yourself moving through the day with no recollection of what you should be doing? Or where you should be going? Just completely coasting through, hoping that nobody notices your unusual behaviour.

It was a Monday; life had resumed to some form of normality and I was back at work unprepared to take on the week. Every menial task felt like a chore; the entire day became such a traumatic experience. I loved my job, but all the energy and enthusiasm that came so naturally had disappeared.

My parents busy Sunday schedule meant I had yet to explain my trip and the outcome. I was relieved. An early dash that morning allowed me to avoid the topic for a while longer; I was biding my time.

The drive to work had been slow; traffic was exceptionally light at 7 am. I stopped for a coffee along the way, hoping it would breathe some life into my exhausted frame. The night's sleep had not been fulfilling, the constant crying had kept me up most of the night and every time I managed to fall asleep, the nightmares soon brought me back to reality. My morning routine had required spending an extra 20 minutes on my face so I could look presentable to some extent.

My façade at work was beginning to fade. My work

colleagues had more intuition than I gave them credit for. A double glance here and there, a sympathetic smile. Although they had absolutely no idea why I wasn't my usual self, they sympathised anyway. It was challenging trying to pretend; I was slowly driving myself insane. I didn't have any interest in knowing how someone's weekend had been or where they went to eat. I knew they would only reciprocate the questions and how did I reply, saying I was okay when in reality, I was the furthest thing from okay.

I almost managed to navigate the entire day before the cracks started to show. I sat at my desk with a tissue in hand, swiping away tear after tear as they fell, hoping that no one else could see. I did not wish to be pitied.

Just as I thought I had caught the last tear, Diane Hardy walked into my office. Diane was an architect with similar credentials to my father; she had been in the industry for a long time and had a wealth of experience. Diane hadn't changed her appearance in the slightest over the years. She still rocked the same 80's hairstyle, the same pinstripe suit and small rectangular glasses that sat neatly at the end of her nose. I had to give her credit; she didn't care what other people thought. She was a true professional who came to work, did her job and then hurried off home to her *'wonderful'* husband and two children as she often described them.

I admired Diane. After 15 long years of service, she was the cornerstone of the firm. Diane lingered at the door, my distress noticeable.

"Hi, Kacy. Are you okay, sweetie?"

She had a soothing voice that instantly made you feel comfortable in her presence.

"Hi Diane, I'll be fine."

I lowered my head slightly to hide the tears.

"Sorry to barge in on you like this. Should I come back?"

"No, honestly, it's fine. I will be okay. Can I help you with something?"

I wanted the exchange over with as quickly and painfully as possible.

"I was just hoping you could show me how to work the new system on my office computer. I can't seem to get my head around it and I know you young kids are all about technology these days. It's no rush, though; whenever you are free would be great."

Her smile was genuine and considerate. I am sure she felt awful for asking a favour when she could see I was upset, so I quickly reassured her that it was not a problem at all.

"Of course. Can I just finish with this email? I'll be right up."

It was not the first time I had helped someone with a computer system. We had an IT department, but in recent weeks I had become a secondary option.

"Honestly, you are a superstar. I owe you a coffee."

"I think you owe me three coffees. I'm going to start keeping tabs."

She laughed, which in turn made me smile, a facial expression I had yet to use since returning from Cannon Beach. She loitered for a moment before speaking again.

"Can I ask something, Kacy?"

"Sure, go ahead."

"If the reason you are upset is because of a girl, then please allow me to give you a few words of advice?"

Was Diane a psychic? I thought. This ought to be interesting.

"Okay, fire away."

She walked over to the window as if pondering how she could say what she wanted to in a way that would resonate. She found her words and turned back towards me; what she said next brought a tear to my eye.

"You are a beautiful, smart, ambitious young lady. Bright stars like you don't wait around for anyone. One day you will find someone that loves you for you and would never see those tears fall from your eyes. Starting today, you need to forget the past, appreciate everything you still have and most definitely look forward to all the amazing things that will undoubtedly come in your future. You are young, your life is just beginning, and those tears you cry right now will only make you stronger. I have lived long enough to know this."

I stood from behind my desk, saying nothing. Instead, I embraced Diane with open arms. A woman I only knew briefly from work. She had taken the time to give me strong words of advice, she had no idea what I was going through, but she did it anyway.

"Thank you so much, Diane. That's really kind of you."

"That is alright, my dear. You know where I am if you ever need to talk. I have been on this planet for 58 years. I guess you could say I have enough knowledge to last another 58 years. I am more than happy to share it with you, anytime you wish."

"Thank you."

"No problem, I'll see you upstairs whenever you're ready."

Diane had been a mystery when I started at the firm. Over time I found out she had been a school teacher for ten years before becoming an author, publishing several universally recognised novels around education before she eventually studied to be an architect. I made it my aim in that moment to get to know Diane more; after all, her words had filled me with a sense of optimism.

I arrived home shortly after 6 pm. Dodging my parents that morning had been simple, but I would not get away with it again. It was time to tell them everything. The house was strangely quiet when I entered, unusual for a Monday evening. Jason always had his friends over for a pizza and gaming night after football practice, but there were no obnoxious boys running through the house or wolf-whistling at me as I walked through the door. I figured it must have been cancelled.

"Kacy, is that you?"

The angelic voice of my mother only ever came out when she wanted something.

"Yes, Mom, 2 seconds."

I hung my coat up and kicked off my shoes in the usual place. After plastering on my happy face, I made my way through to the kitchen. Dad was too enthralled in the football to even realise I had entered the house. My mother, on the other hand, was more than eager to embrace me before I even had a chance to drop my bag on the kitchen counter.

"So, how was work? I imagine you must be in a great mood after this weekend's events?"

Not quite, if she only knew. The conversation would be painful, but she had to know.

"Work was okay, the usual. I actually need to talk to you about this weekend."

She put her hand up as if she already knew what I was going to say.

"If it's about Alex coming over here for Christmas, then you know that is okay with your father and me. I know she only has her sister now, and that can't be easy for her. Natalie is welcome to come too if she doesn't have any plans."

I was beyond confused. Why would she just assume Alex would come for Christmas? My face dropped, the ripping of my heart almost audible.

"What are you talking about?"

"Well, I have no problem with her now that the two of you

have worked out your differences. I'm happy for you, darling. We had a good talk about it earlier today."

My jaw hit the floor. Surely she meant my father.

"Wait. What? Talked with who?"

Michelle Sullivan had lost the plot. The only plausible explanation. She rolled her eyes.

"Well, Alex, of course. Don't get upset though; I didn't cross any lines. I was extremely calm as if nothing had happened. I knew you wouldn't want me to discuss your relationship without you being there."

She had to be kidding me. Was this a prank? My initial thought. My mom was a terrible liar and her face was sincere, not a hint of fabrication.

"Alex was here? This afternoon? Like right here in our house?"

My heart began beating out of my chest at an unprecedented rate.

"Yes, Alex. You know the one you flew to Oregon for? Are you feeling okay, sweetie?"

"I am aware of who she is, Mom. I am just a little surprised, that's all. What did she say?"

Was I dreaming? A little surprised was the understatement of the century.

"She told me to give you this piece of paper, before you ask; I didn't read it. I still don't understand why she can't just text you. I figured you would be able to shed some light on that."

I was staring at my mom, then at the piece of paper in her hand, unresponsive to anything she had just said since it registered that Alex had been in our home earlier that day.

"I think her phones broken…anyway, Mom, I need to to…erm…go."

I hurled my bag from the counter back over my shoulder, took the letter from my mom's outstretched hand and headed for the stairs.

"Wait, honey, what do you want for dinner? Will Alex be joining us?"

I almost replied, *'In all honesty, Michelle, I have no idea what Alex is doing'* but I refrained from the lippy response.

"I don't know, Mom."

Food was the last thing on my mind. I threw my bag on the floor and carefully took a seat on the edge of my bed; the suspense was killing me. I felt a sudden sense of déjà vu. The last letter I had opened from Alex filled me with a sudden surge of pain. Would this one be the same?

At first glance, it seemed short and sweet.

Kacy,

I couldn't make sense of the note you left. Jennifer ripped it into pieces before I even had a chance to read it. All I know is that I had to come back for you. There was nothing left for me in Oregon; my life is with you here in Raleigh. If you will still have me, that is.

There is so much we need to talk about and so much I need to explain. I didn't get your number from the piece of paper you left hence why I am writing this note. I will come to your house around 8 pm this evening.

I love you.

Alex

It was 7 pm. Alex would be at my house in less than an hour. I didn't have time to process the letter, she was in Raleigh and she was coming to my house, in that moment, that was all that mattered. It took me 15 minutes to shower, fix my hair up into a ponytail and apply a thin layer of tinted moisturiser to give off a sun-kissed, smooth-skinned glow. I threw on some sweatpants and a tight t-shirt, opting for the comfortable, natural look. A quick spray of perfume and I was as presentable as I could be with the time given. I eyed the bedside clock as it ticked closer to 8. I had a few minutes to come to terms with the reality of it all. The shower had given me some alone time with my thoughts; I now had several to consider.

Alex had not seen my phone number, which left me with only one clear-cut assumption. Jennifer Locksley. It made sense; of course it did.

Alex still loved me. She said it right there in the letter; she had flown back to Raleigh to be with me. That made me the happiest I had ever been.

There was a third and final pressing thought. Did I tell her about Lara? There was a sudden pang of guilt when I thought or said her name aloud. I knew that I hadn't done anything wrong; me and Alex were broken up. Besides, she had been seeing Jennifer, which kind of made things even, but there was one point of difference. Lara was now my friend and I didn't want to lose her. She had become a part of my life that I was not sure I could live without. I knew without any doubt that I loved Alex, that she was the one I wanted to spend the rest of my life with, but Lara was someone I did not want to compromise. The only way I could figure it all out would be to come clean, to tell Alex everything.

Surely, she would understand? The doorbell chimed, taking me away from my many thoughts to just the one. Alex.

CHAPTER EIGHTEEN

There she stood, in the doorway to my bedroom, a silhouette of perfection. So unreal to me that I had to make sure I was not dreaming. Neither of us knew what to say, who should speak first, I was not entirely sure. Just having her stood before me, knowing she had flown back to be with me, was enough. The silence was broken when Alex spoke.

"Your mom let me in."

"I can't believe you are here."

I whispered. She walked forward and closed the door gently behind her.

"Kacy..."

"Alex…"

I gestured for her to continue first.

"Please forgive me for everything. I should have known you wouldn't just leave me and now I feel ridiculous that I ever doubted you. If I could go back and do it all differently, I would. I feel like a complete idiot; it all makes perfect sense now."

She edged another step towards me.

"I know it wasn't your fault; we were both more naive than we care to admit. Jennifer's scheme played out perfectly, really, didn't it."

Alex shook her head.

"No, it didn't because I am here now. Despite everything, I am here."

Alex smiled proudly.

"I am sorry too, by the way. I am sorry that I didn't come sooner to try and work things out. I found it hard to believe that you would hurt me like that, but I guess when the evidence mounted up, I was too heartbroken to believe otherwise."

"I know. I understand."

She edged closer again.

"What happened on Saturday? Why didn't you come back like you said you would?"

She sighed. I had even missed the way she sighed.

"I tried to come back. Jennifer just proved difficult. I tried to shake her so many times. When I got back to my house, eventually, she found your note before I did and tore it to pieces. I couldn't find a phone number to let you know what was going on."

It became immediately apparent who did find my phone number.

"So, I imagine Jennifer took my phone number then based on the text I received at the airport?"

Alex shook her head in disbelief.

"Well, it certainly wasn't me, so whatever was said, don't believe a word. She is unbelievable; I thought I had talked some sense into her after what Charlotte told me. Can you believe I thought she was a nice girl? I was willing to try and help her."

Alex ran her fingers through her hair, disbelief apparent in her frown.

"I can believe that she probably comes across like a *'nice'* girl when she wants to. We are the unfortunate ones that had to learn the hard way. What do you mean? What did Charlotte tell you? That's her sister, right?"

Neither of us had moved from our standing positions. I had visions of running into her arms, embracing after so many months apart, but there was still a minor uncertainty in my approach.

"Yes, Charlotte is her sister. I won't bore you with the details today, but she said some things that made me rethink Jennifer's intentions. I gave her the benefit of the doubt. I was even willing to forgive her if she could just be honest and admit her mistakes. I thought I'd got through to her, but then when I said I was leaving to come back to Raleigh, the atmosphere changed again. That must have been when she sent you the text message."

Alex looked down at her feet, the frustration evident. The encounters with Jennifer would be tales for another day. As much as I wanted to know, the need to kiss her was greater.

"Is that why you didn't come and look for me? I know it sounds cliché, but I sat in the airport hoping you would come running in at the last minute. When you didn't, and I received that text, I genuinely thought it was the end for us…again."

Alex stepped forward; she stood less than one metre in front of me. I was the most vulnerable I had ever been. The woman before me could make or break my universe in an instant.

"I'm sorry that I wasn't there. When I got to the airport, I looked everywhere, but I was too late. I found the departures board, and there was only one plane to Raleigh, and it had already boarded. So, I booked on the next available flight out, which was early this morning."

My brain would not register anything other than the longing for her touch. When her eyes locked with mine, it sent a shiver through my entire body.

"How did you end up here with my mom? I thought she'd lost the plot when she told me."

Alex reached out for my hand. I relished her touch.

"I didn't know where else to go. I just assumed you would be at home. I think it was more wishful thinking. When your mom answered the door and said you were at work, I was stuck. I could tell immediately you hadn't told her anything about the weekend because she was oblivious. She assumed we must be back together because I'd turned up."

My eyes focused on her lips as she spoke; we were close now. I could see the rise and fall of her chest. The slight smirk that appeared when she noticed I was fixated made my heart race.

"So, you just waltzed in and played happy families for an hour?"

We both laughed at the concept.

"I guess you could say that. You know me, I just went with the flow. She made me a coffee, we had a quick conversation and I left. She was extremely polite to me considering everything; I was surprised."

My hands weaved in and out of Alex's with ease, finding their way once again.

"She has always liked you, Alex."

Our conversation was reduced to that of a whisper. I wanted to feel her lips on mine once again. The brief silence exposed my irregular breathing; she had an undeniable effect on me.

"I love you, Kacy. I don't know what else there is to say that matters."

I needed her; I wanted her, uncontrollably in that moment. I yearned for everything to go back to the way it was supposed to be.

"I love you too, Alex."

There were no words spoken that would ring more true. I looked deep into her penetrating blue eyes and for the briefest of moments, time stood still. The anticipation of her lips on mine was so intense I forgot to breathe. The sudden urge of desire racing through my veins was overwhelming. I felt it everywhere.

Finally, she pulled me in close. The kiss I had been craving softly upon my lips, so overpowering, like nothing I had ever experienced. The taste of her lips, the texture, the movement, it all came flooding back. Alex pulled me in at the waist and held the nape of my neck firmly. I was bursting with a passion that I had forgotten existed.

"Wait…are you sure...don't you want to talk about..."

I forced my lips back upon hers. The time for talking had surpassed.

"No more talking…not now."

The rawness and intensity in that moment had me on cloud nine.

"Lock the door."

I pushed Alex back towards the bedroom door, my lips freely kissing her lips, then down to her neck and back. Once I felt Alex's back touch the door, I reached through and flicked the lock all the way to the right. We needed some privacy. We fumbled our way back towards the bed. I had never wanted anything as much in my whole life. Piece by piece, our clothing fell to the floor, first my top, her jacket, my sweats, her jeans, until finally there was nothing left. The smoothness of her naked body lying over mine evoked pure sensation.

We had made love in the past, but that time was undeniably different. There was a ferocious need for one another, an incredible, overpowering desire to feel her body upon mine, to feel her lips caressing every inch of my naked figure. I wrapped my legs securely around Alex's bare waist as she lifted me to sit directly in her lap. She caressed my neck, slowly moving down my back with such delicate touches. She pulled away just enough to look deep into my eyes.

"I have never wanted anyone or anything as much in my life."

My heart ached for her; I ached to take away the guilt I could see hidden behind her words. Guilt that was not hers to feel. I would show her that none of it was her fault. I would show her just how much I loved her, more than words could ever explain.

"Show me."

We lay side by side for some time, so intimate and so complete now that we had each other again. Each kiss afterwards brought with it a wave of ecstasy. I lay in her arms, hoping and praying that the future would be kind to us. That I could dream of a world where Alex was the only person I would ever kiss. She was it for me; she was my definition of true love. I could say I knew what it felt like to love someone with every ounce of your being.

Alex moved the hair away from my eyes as we lay peacefully in each other's arms.

"What? What are you thinking?"

She made me nervous.

"I am thinking about how lucky I am to be lying next to the most beautiful girl in the world. You are the envy of all women, do you know that?"

She flattered me.

"Don't be silly. You are only saying that because you just got lucky."

I nudged her playfully. It felt so good to be by her side, to hear her laughter, as if no time had passed.

"I did get extremely lucky, in many ways, but in all seriousness. I should have never let you go so easily, Kace. I was just so hurt and with everything that happened with Rose. I am just so happy that we found each other again. I don't ever want to be without you."

A small tear formed in the corner of my eye as I saw just how meaningful every word was. The subject of Rose had been one we had not yet broached. I knew it would be sensitive, and I had waited for her to bring it up rather than pry.

"Do you want to talk about Rose? I know we haven't had the chance yet. We don't have to. I just want you to know how sorry I am that I couldn't be there with you."

I could only hope that it was peaceful. She had been an amazing woman who brought so much light to the lives of the people who knew her.

"I haven't come to terms with it all, to be honest, so it's still difficult to talk about. She knew it was coming; I think we all did. She went from surviving all odds to being so sick in the space of a week, and then she was gone. It caught up with her so suddenly."

There would be a void in Alex that no person or materialistic item would ever fill. The same void that appeared when she lost her parents, except it was deeper, darker, and full of unimaginable grief that would take time to reduce but never fully heal.

"I am so sorry, Alex."

I held her even tighter.

"Me and Nat made her as happy as we could, in the end. She made that clear, and we carry that with us all the time now. We did right by her and that is all we could have done, so don't worry, I take peace from that."

Alex's strength was admirable.

"I promise to always be there for you in the future, through whatever life throws at us. I will never let you down again, Alex."

She smiled, her fingertips traced the length of my cheekbone as she tilted my head to place a kiss on my lips once again. Her kisses were like a drug; I was the addict, completely and utterly addicted to her. I wondered if she understood the intoxicating effect she had on me. There was not one solitary thing I could say or do that would justifiably explain it. I could only hope that over time I could prove that I was worthy of her.

"Marry me?"

"Huh?"

I froze, almost certain I had interpreted the words clearly, but the embarrassment of being wrong would be too much to bear.

"I know it might sound crazy, but the moment I met you, I knew my life would never be the same. I am not the person I want to be without you. I know that the past few months have been hard. I know that we have only known each other for a short time, but you are it for me, Kacy. I know it with every inch of my heart."

I remained silent, still unsure whether or not she meant it.

"Rose told me that the moment I knew I could not live without someone was the moment I needed to make them mine forever. I cannot live without you, Kacy. So please, I promise you, right here, right now, that if you say yes, I will spend the rest of my life making you happy. Nothing will ever come between us again."

She paused.

"So, will you marry me?"

It felt sudden, but deep within my soul, I wanted nothing more than to spend the rest of my life with her. The shock was momentarily paralyzing, not because I didn't want to marry her, but because I did not expect the incredible woman laid beside me to propose.

That morning, I had been regrettably single and devastatingly heartbroken with no clear path to revival. Fast forward 12 hours and the love of my life was asking me to marry her. What an unpredictable turn of events. My life had gone from utter chaos to picture-perfect harmony. All thanks to Alex Dawson.

There was no response I would allow to slip from my lips other than the one I sincerely intended to express. The one that would start my life with the woman I loved, a life and a love I could have only dreamed of. It felt there and then like the beauty in our scars had prevailed.

With that being said, I seized the day.

"Yes. I will marry you, Alex Dawson."

TWO YEARS LATER

"Lara, you made it."

I was so delighted to see my best friend; it had been a month since she left Raleigh to travel around America.

"Well, I just had to come back for this crazy housewarming party. I heard the guest list was super exclusive."

She looked great, rejuvenated. Her long blonde hair had been cut just below her ears. It was wavy and textured, very surfer-girl; I loved it. I reached out to touch her hair in approval.

"You look incredible. Seriously, this hairstyle is doing things for you."

I pulled her in for the biggest embrace I could conjure.

"Well, the ladies seem to like it."

She ran her fingers through her hair, humorously showing me her model pose.

"I bet they do. It's honestly so good to see you."

There were only two people in the world that made me smile as though my face would split; the other one was my fiancée.

"It's so good to see you too, Kace."

We had so much catching up to do.

"When will you be starting back at the bar? I know Alex misses you."

Lara had taken a manager's job at Alex's bar one year prior. Alex and Natalie's focus had turned towards the second bar they were opening. The plan was to open two or three bars in Raleigh, then branch out. They wanted someone they could trust, and Lara had been fed up with her current job and wanted a change of scenery. It had all worked out perfectly.

"As soon as possible. I won't be able to afford the rent on that apartment otherwise. Thank you again for that. I owe you one, Kace."

Alex and I had decided it was time to get a bigger place. As much as I had grown to love the apartment, I wanted a garden and guest bedrooms—a house we could make our own. Alex was reluctant to let the apartment go, so renting it out seemed like the better choice. I had immediately asked Lara, giving her first refusal. It was the perfect apartment for a young, single person and the ideal location.

"What are best friends for?"

"Don't let Whitney hear you say that. Where is that red-headed bombshell anyway."

Whitney was making herself useful in the kitchen. The caterers were regularly hired by her parents, so she knew exactly what food to order and how it would best be presented.

"She's in the kitchen pretending to help, although all I see is her bossing everyone around whilst drinking her Pornstar Martini."

"Standard Whitney then. When do you want to discuss the apartment anyway?"

"We can discuss it tomorrow. You are staying here tonight anyway, so we will discuss it over breakfast. How does that sound?"

The smell from the kitchen was to die for.

"Are you sure? I agreed to crash at Jessica's for a few days until I got sorted."

"You are my best friend and I won't take no for an answer. Why do you think I got a house with two guest bedrooms? One for you and one for Whitney, obviously."

She grinned.

"I did wonder, actually; I hope I got the biggest one?"

Lara knew better than that.

"You went travelling, so Whitney got first pick. She even brought some pyjama's, slippers, a candle, her favourite moisturiser, and some perfume, amongst other things. You know, just so that she has some supplies. I fear I won't get rid of her."

She laughed hysterically at the prospect.

"How's it going with her boyfriend anyway? The last time I called her, they had fallen out. I don't want to bring it up if it's a sore subject."

That was a story for another day.

"Well, he's not here tonight, so what does that tell you?"

I assumed. I didn't expect to see him again anytime soon.

"Roger that. Note to self, don't mention the boyfriend."

Whitney never seemed to surpass the six-month mark; it was a mystery to me.

"Anyway, why don't you go and mingle. Everyone is in the lounge; it was supposed to be a low-key housewarming party, but it got a little out of hand."

She laughed as she put her arm casually around my shoulder.

"I have missed you so much. Travelling the country isn't fun without my partner in crime."

"I have missed you more. Raleigh has not been the same without you. Next time you decide to take off, do you think you could just make it a weekend break? That I could live with."

Her response, a smile that melted my heart.

"Or you could just come with me next time."

The option was a welcome one. Lara looked around for someone in particular.

"Where's Alex? I want to hear all about the new bar."

"She was in the garden with Natalie last time I saw her. Honestly, you have to see it. We could go tomorrow. It's amazing."

I edged towards the bar; hosting had meant the alcohol levels in my system were a lot lower than everyone else's. Most of the guests had arrived, so it was time to enjoy the evening.

"Head out and find her. I'm going to grab a drink. I'll bring you one over, Bourbon and Coke?"

"Always."

Lara winked, her eyes sparkled. It was a wonder she was single.

Life had been kind to me. Alex Dawson was my fiancée, and we had just bought our first home. We never spoke of Cannon Beach unless it was from a place of happiness. The pain endured had made us both more appreciative of the love we shared. My relationship with Lara had gone from strength to strength, she had been brought into my life for a reason still undiscovered, but there were no reservations. The bond she had formed with Alex brought me pure joy. Any jealousy that had materialised swiftly disappeared when I made it clear I would choose no sides. I had the best family, the best group of friends and the woman I loved beyond all measure and reason.

Perfection is unattainable, but we build our lives based on what we choose. We have the power to obtain the most remarkable things in life, but nothing will ever be greater than the love of another human. I loved, and I was loved in return; that was my idea of perfection.

Author Biography

Nicole Spencer-Skillen is a number 1 best-selling author of Lesbian Romance and Fiction. Originally from Lancashire, England. She is 28 years old and happily married to her wife of 2 years. She has spent the last decade writing quotes, short stories and LGBT novels recreationally. When she is not writing, you will find her travelling the world, doing endless HIIT workouts or relaxing at home with her 2 dogs whilst dreaming up her next novel.

Lesbian romance is a genre Nicole is incredibly passionate about and she would love nothing more than to make an impact within this area. Growing up, she did not see herself represented in the books she read or in the book industry as a whole. Therefore, she predominantly read heterosexual romance novels, which happen to be some of her favourite books of all time, but they lacked the emotional pull she needed as she didn't feel she could fully resonate with the characters. That is why her aim is to write books that the LGBT+ community can connect with.

Nicole believes her writing to be real, honest and modern, but most importantly relatable. Her main aim is to appeal to the LGBT audience; the people who are looking for inspiration, especially the younger generation of gay women. She wants them to be able to see themselves in a book and resonate wholly with the characters and feel the realness of them as they read it.

Fun facts about Nicole, if she could live anywhere in the world it would be New York City. The city of dreams. Her favourite book is The Notebook by Nicholas Sparks of which she proudly owns a first edition. Her favourite sport is basketball, she proudly supports the Los Angeles Lakers and religiously watch's every game. She has a passion for quotes, as you would expect after studying some of the most famous quotes throughout history. The one that resonates with her the most, is actually very simple.

"You miss 100% of the shots you don't take."

If you want to get to know her more, follow her on Instagram account @nss_writings.

Printed in Great Britain
by Amazon